Architectural Design

THE 1970s IS HERE AND NOW

Guest-edited by Samantha Hardingham

Architectural Design
Vol 75 No 2 March/April 2005

Editorial Offices
International House
Ealing Broadway Centre
London W5 5DB
T: +44 (0)20 8326 3800
F: +44 (0)20 8326 3801
E: architecturaldesign@wiley.co.uk

Editor
Helen Castle

Editorial and Design Management
Mariangela Palazzi-Williams

Art Direction/Design
Christian Küsters (CHK Design)

Design Assistant
Hannah Dumphy (CHK Design)

**Project Coordinator
and Picture Editor**
Caroline Ellerby

Advertisement Sales
01243 843272

Editorial Board
Will Alsop, Denise Bratton, Adriaan
Beukers, André Chaszar, Peter
Cook, Teddy Cruz, Max Fordham,
Massimiliano Fuksas, Edwin
Heathcote, Anthony Hunt, Charles
Jencks, Jan Kaplicky, Robert
Maxwell, Jayne Merkel, Monica
Pidgeon, Antoine Predock,
Michael Rotondi, Leon van Schaik,
Ken Yeang

Contributing Editors
André Chaszar
Craig Kellogg
Jeremy Melvin
Jayne Merkel

ISBN 047001136X
Profile No 174

Abbreviated positions:
b=bottom, c=centre, l=left, r=right

Front cover illustration: © John Walter.

ΔD
pp 6, 7, 8(t&br), 9(bl&bc) © Will McLean; p 8(bl)
© FoeBuD eV, photo Peter Ehrentraut; p 9(t) ©
Paul Purgas; p 9(c) © Tim Lucas/Price & Myers
3D Engineering; p 9(br) © Howard Barlow; p
10(tl) courtesy Dunlop Transcalm, photo Chris
Logan; p 10(tr) courtesy Worldwide Project
Consortium; p 10(b) © Arup; p 11 © Nolle IUT
GmbH; p 17(t&b) © Samantha Hardingham; p
17(c) © Archigram Archive; pp 20–7 © Nicholas
Lister; pp 28-33 courtesy James Madge; p 35
(top 7 images) courtesy John Frazer; p 35 (c) ©
David Greene; p 35 (bl) © Julia Frazer; p 35(br)
©Suha Bekki, courtesy Archigram Archive; p 36
courtesy John Frazer; pp 37-43 © John Frazer;
pp 44-7 © S333 Architecture & Urbanism; pp
48-9 © Peter de Kan; pp 51-2 © Gutierrez +
Portefaix; p 53 © Lou Linwei/Sinopix; p 55 ©
Richard Jones/Sinopix; pp 56-7 © Jason Lowe;
pp 58-9 © muf architecture/art; pp 60–65 © Nic
Clear; p 66 © Neil Spiller; p 68 © Violette
Cornelius; p 69 © Jon Goodbun; p 70 courtesy
Richard Cochrane; p 72 © Richard Rogers
Partnership/Eamon O'Mahony; p 73(t) © Antony
Turner; p 73(c&b) courtesy Robert Webb; p 74,
75(t), 76-7 © Robert Webb/XCO2; p 75(c&b) ©
Niall McLaughlin Architects; pp 78-81 © John
Vincent, photos John Vincent and Flora
Gardens; pp 82-7 © Collection FRAC Centre,
Orléans, France; pp 88-9 © Marion Clayfield
and David De Sousa; p 90(t) © Maggie Smith; p
90(bl&r) © Gary Doherty; p 91© Peter
Aaron/Esto; p 92(t) © Victoria Watson; p 92(bl)
© Populararchitecture; p 92(br) © noodleJam
2004; p 93(b) © Miki Inamura; p 95 © bceeg.

ΔD+
PP 98–100 © Frederick Charles; pp 101–02 ©
Bevk Perovic arhitekti, photo B Zupan; p 103 &
105 (bottom 3 images) © Bevk Perovic arhitek
ti, photos M Paternoster; p 105 (top 3 images) ©
Bevk Perovic arhitekti, photos M Kambic; pp
106-07 © Bevk Perovic arhitekti; pp 108–13 ©
HLT A/S; pp 114–17 © Archer Architects; pp
118–19, 120(t&c), 121(r) & 122(t) © realities:
united, Berlin, 2003; p 120(b) © Landesmuseum
Joanneum, Graz, 2003; pp 121(l) & 122(b) ©
Harry Schiffer, Graz, 2003; pp 123–4 courtesy
Lonsdale; p 125 © Martin Charles.

Subscription Offices UK
John Wiley & Sons Ltd.
Journals Administration Department
1 Oldlands Way, Bognor Regis
West Sussex, PO22 9SA
T: +44 (0)1243 843272
F: +44 (0)1243 843232
E: cs-journals@wiley.co.uk

Printed in Italy by Conti Tipocolor.
All prices are subject to change
without notice.
[ISSN: 0003-8504]

ΔD is published bimonthly and is available
to purchase on both a subscription basis
and as individual volumes at the following
prices.

Single Issues
Single issues UK: £22.50
Singles issues outside UK: US$45.00
Details of postage and packing charges
available on request.

Annual Subscription Rates 2005
Institutional Rate
Print only or Online only: UK £175/US$290
Combined Print and Online: UK £193/US$320
Personal Rate
Print only: UK£99/US$155
Student Rate
Print only: UK£70/US$110

Prices are for six issues and include
postage and handling charges. Periodicals
postage paid at Jamaica, NY 11431. Air
freight and mailing in the USA by
Publications Expediting Services Inc, 200
Meacham Avenue, Elmont, NY 11003

Individual rate subscriptions must be paid
by personal cheque or credit card.
Individual rate subscriptions may not be
resold or used as library copies.

Postmaster
Send address changes to ΔD Publications
Expediting Services, 200 Meacham Avenue,
Elmont, NY 11003

THE 1970s IS HERE AND NOW

Guest-edited by Samantha Hardingham

AD

A rose-tinted, nostalgic approximation of 1970s culture is piped to us through television, fashion retail and glossy magazines: whether TV favourites such as 'Morecambe and Wise' or 'The Magic Roundabout', or the replication of curvy, orange and shag-pile interiors. In its exaggerations, this evocation of everything 1970s veers between stereotypes of all things hippyish and joyfully lurid. Our lens is often so misted up with this retro-mania that it is difficult to remember what the inheritance of that decade really was for architecture and design, in terms of ideas and thinking. What Samantha Hardingham, the guest-editor of this issue, has so insightfully done is to revive the spirit and modus operandi of ⌂ in that era. (Her method comes out of an intimate knowledge and affection for ⌂ during this decade, which was furthered by research into the work of Cedric Price, completed with him just before his death.) By pulling together patchworks of current information and views, Hardingham has worked – albeit with the aid of the Internet, Word and email – just as Monica Pidgeon and her technical editors might have done in the first half of the decade. She has triumphantly revived Peter Murray's and Cedric Price's Cosmorama! Thus the 1970s becomes a film, or filter, by which we view the present. This brings into focus just how many of the major architectural preoccupations remain the same, even if the content has shifted rapidly – architectural form, technique and surface appearance having moved on with great alacrity in the ensuing decades. For architecture's obsessions with technology, information and the environment were first prefigured in the pages of Pidgeon's ⌂ magazine of the late 1960s and early 1970s. The seemingly random manner in which this was also compiled, dictated by the printer's grid, also foreshadowed the Web; the spontaneity of the issues belying the rigorous and thoroughly dynamic, curating and editing process. (Hardingham describes in her essay how Pidgeon discovered a printer in Middlesbrough who was able to print in colour in a single afternoon.) Just as John Frazer states in his article that ⌂'s raison d'être in the 1970s was the coming together of advancing technology and comment – the same, I hope, could also be said of ⌂ today.

COSMORAMA

The inspirational Cosmorama as it appeared in July 1970. The image is of a blow-up mirrored dome designed by Chrysalis (Chris Dawson, Alan Stanton, David MacDermott and Rob Sangster – many of whom moved to Paris soon after this event to work on the architectural design team for the Centre Pompidou). The dome epitomises the ambidextrous embrace with which architects tackled their art at the time – from idea to application. The caption that accompanied the image was as follows: 'The mirrored dome (similar to that constructed for the Pepsi-Cola pavilion at Osaka [Worlds Fair, 1970]) used in the filming of *Myra Breckinridge*. The dome formed the background for two sequences, one in the operating theatre (in which it is reported to have disturbed Raquel Welch, who dislikes profile shots and reflections) and one in a nightclub (in which Mae West enjoyed herself hugely).'

The agenda for architectural discourse in the 1970s was clearly set in the 1960s. One decade moved seamlessly into the next, and indeed swelled to a crescendo of realism, idealism and pluralism by the mid-1970s, only to shift abruptly to a more linear pace with the onset of Postmodernism. The pages of Δ at the time, specifically the Cosmorama section, tracked (and in many ways determined) the profundity of the moment in both architectural and publishing terms. This issue celebrates the platform that the magazine (as it was then) afforded its contributors, and how its legacy might serve to inspire subsequent generations of architect thinkers. It aims to capture the memories of past contributors in a contemporary context, and with the advantage of the generation and information gap hopes to inspire new areas of investigation with a particular emphasis on the value of publishing a wealth of ideas. Δ

A COSMORAMA OF NOW

Cosmorama defined both ⏁ and the spirit of the times during the late 1960s and early 1970s. Its fantastically diverse range of technically orientated contributions were sent in from all over the world and served as a rich resource for generations of students and practising architects. **Will McLean** has been inspired to trawl for more contributions ever since reading the bound copies whilst studying architecture during the late 1980s. These are some of his most recent ones.

Chewing the Fat – Dashboard Dining

The standard metropolitan Deskfast consisting of an imported 'ready to bake' pastry, industrial coffee with optional milk and sachet sugar, and obligatory bottled water.

While the Lincolnshire town of Melton Mowbray digests news of new government directives (known as the Fat Tax), which may outlaw the pork pie, consider for a moment the prospect of breathable food. Polemically explored in Spanish designer Marti Guixe's Pharma Food project, 'neutriceuticals' or 'functional foods' are part of a growing range of function-specific foodstuffs including cholesterol-reducing margarine, energy drinks and a melatonin-rich milk that helps you sleep. In its breathable form one wonders how easy it may be to overeat or inadvertently inhale somebody else's lunch. More prosaically we consider the new cultural indicator that is Deskfast, a workstation-specific food opportunity which, according to Humfrey Hunter of the London *Evening Standard*, has become the new morning meal for more than a quarter of London's office workers and, along with the growth in portable breakfasts, has replaced morning meals at home. These movable feasts are viewed by some as a threat to the designated food break and are currently being challenged by the Trades Union Congress (TUC) and its Scottish counterpart in a new joint initiative to cut back on unpaid overtime entitled 'Work Your Proper Hours Day'.

Space Syntax Food

How better to study the movement of fellow human beings than through that most analogue of tracking devices – discarded chewing gum? Margins of error have to be built-in for the unplanned transportation of the exhausted data morsels on one's shoes. We are, however, living in the halcyon days of long-life synthetic rubber with added softeners, sweeteners and flavourings, more commonly described as chewing or bubble gum. A recent government select committee received written evidence from Wrigley's, which dominates the market with a 90 per cent share and has invested £5 million over the past five years into producing a more easily removable gum. The London Borough of Westminster has an average of 20 pieces of gum per square metre, and its removal by steam cleaning or freeze treatments is expensive and slow. Professor Cosgrove at Bristol University has been developing a less sticky substrate, but biodegradable gum is the panacea. The Department for Environment Food and Rural Affairs (Defra) recently described gum as the most geographically prolific littered item in the UK, appearing in 94 per cent of 100,000 surveyed sites in 50 local authorities. Chewing gum was outlawed in Singapore in 1992; it has recently become available again in Singapore chemists, reclassified as therapeutic or medicinal gum it can be purchased on production of ID and on supply of home address.

The hazards of inappropriately disposed gum, welded to a Commando sole.

The Internet of Things

The electronic product code (FPC) was launched in Chicago in 2003 as the successor to the barcode. 'An open technology infrastructure, this network will use radio frequency identification devices (RFIDS) enabling machines to sense man-made objects anywhere in the world.' It is described as 'an internet of things' by Kevin Ashton, executive director of the Auto-ID centre at MIT. Go to Google 'Object Search' (if it has not arrived yet it is on its way), and type in 'piece of wood' or 'lump' or, more specifically, measurements and generic/material type, and you will be supplied with a map reference, zip code and/or supplier. This souped-up barcode not only tells you what an object is, where and who manufactured it, but also, through a network of 'readers', whether it is moving. The corporate announcement limits EPC to describing, cataloguing and tracking 'man-made' objects; however, an RFID tag could be fixed to anything, including animals, plants or people, and has generated concerns about the potential for invasions of privacy. Sean Dodson of the *Guardian* newspaper quotes Rob van Kranenburg from the St Joost Academy in the Netherlands: 'Perhaps in a network society we will have to give up the ghost of 19th century notions of privacy.' He then calls for a public debate on an infrastructure that is currently being put in place. 'It is a simple concept with enormous implications,' reads the Auto ID centre. Delta Airlines in the US has recently announced plans to fit RFID tags to luggage, allowing passengers to track their bags, and in Osaka, Japan, the Wakayama Prefecture

Details of a 'passive' RFID tag, the type used in library books.

School has decided to tag its pupils to track their movements. Tags will be fitted in their schoolbags and clothing. A similar 'tagging' type technology is currently being used by the Agricultural Research Service in Tucson, Arizona. Artificial rocks fitted with transponders are being introduced to rivers and are being tracked to study erosion patterns.

Human Computer Interaction

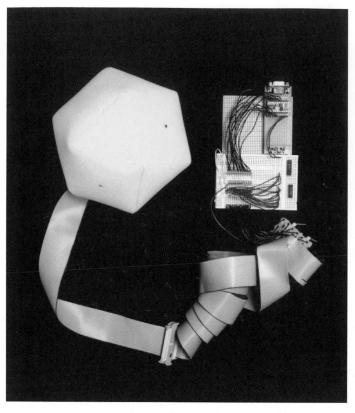

Digital Putty, a prototypical tactile computer interface developed by Stefan Kueppers, Andrew Whiting and Will McLean, 2001.

It is important to note that Nicholas Negroponte's seminal book of 1970, *The Architecture Machine*, was subtitled *Toward a more human environment* and dedicated 'to the first machine that can appreciate the gesture'. Recent research conducted by Dr Tom Buchanan at the University of Westminster has reported that people find it easier to be open and honest with a computer than with fellow humans. This was precisely the effect that Negroponte documents in his account of the 'Hessdorfer Experiment', in which a teleprinter machine was brought into a ghetto area of Boston and residents were invited to talk with the machine about their local environment. The dialogue, although constrained by typewritten text, was fluent and frank in a way that would not have seemed possible in a human–human interaction in the given context. The reality was that the relationship was person to person via an interface, which had the useful side effect of enabling a conversation. Dr Buchanan, quoted in the *Guardian* newspaper in March 2003, said: 'People can sometimes reveal more about themselves to computers than to people, due to an absence of social cues. They don't have to explain themselves or face a fear of disapproval – and people just feel more free.'

The Future In-Store

Protesters at the opening of Metro's Extra Future Store, airing concerns about potential threats to privacy.

The Extra Future Store (part of Metro Group's Future store initiative) in Rheinberg, near Cologne, Germany, has been established as a testbed for new retail technology. As with military technology, so it is with the technology of selling, as new selling systems and stock-tracking technologies will spawn potential products and services within the field of architecture, through typically slow technology transfer. Featured technologies include 'everywhere displays' by IBM, projecting advertisements and promotions that follow you around the store. Veg-Cam is a vegetable recognition system, which prices fruit and vegetables when held aloft. Most controversial is the widespread use of radio frequency identification devices (RFIDS) used to tag the products. Metro has hailed the trials as a success and is extending them to 200 of its other outlets. According to *Retail Week* magazine, Metro's Extra Future Store will see an 'expected reduction in shrinkage of 18%'. 'Shrinkage' is the technical term for shoplifting. However, the use of RFID technology has seen the store picketed by activists protesting about the potential threats to privacy that the trackable tags could engender.

Deployable Structures

Sequence showing the operations of a limited production prototype 'iris' from the Deployable Structures Lab, Cambridge.

Recently highlighted by the American inventor Chuck Hoberman and his incredibly expanding spheres, deployable structures are again being seriously studied and developed by groups like the Deployable Structures Lab (DSL) at Cambridge University. Frank Jensen, who recently completed his doctoral thesis under the supervision of Professor Sergio Pellegrino, has been developing an interesting range of deployable surfaces. Originally a symmetrical 2-D openable 'iris', they have since developed into irregular arrays of linked surfaces that can coalesce into a single plane. Inspired in part by the deployable scissor-hinged Space-Grids of Spanish architect Emilio Perez Pinero, the surfaces have recently become 3-D (curved in two planes). Under investigation as retractable stadium roofs, one cannot help feeling that these wonderful objects might work at a number of different scales. Another excellent resource for operable, deployable or movable structures is the Kinetic Design Group at MIT directed by Michael Fox (see 'Thinkorama' article) who is featured in the recently published *The Art of Portable Architecture* by Jennifer Segal.

Kidnap Servicing

Recent Royal College of Art industrial design graduate Paul Purgas has responded to the 70 per cent rise in global kidnapping rates in the last decade by developing Kidnap Servicing. The package includes a car abduction simulator currently incorporating the back end of a suitably sinister 1970s Mercedes, and a physical training DVD in case of long-term incarceration. He has also developed a series of controllable environments including multidirectional sound systems, a multi-axis treadmill, climatic and atmospheric controls, and a range of low-friction surface inhibitors.

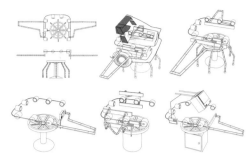

Drawings for the car abduction simulator by designer Paul Purgas.

Developable Surfaces

The developed surfaces of the Arch for Wolfgang and Heron's *Angel Wing* sculpture.

A developable surface is any surface that can be created from a flat plane without creasing, stretching or tearing it: a cone is a good example. Structural engineer Timothy Lucas, of Price and Myers's 3D Engineering group, is successfully using the principles of developable surfaces to structurally design complex geometries in projects like Marks Barfield's Fibonacci Café in Birmingham where a double-curved surface is being clad in flat, twisted panels. The advantage of working with developable surfaces is that by using inexpensive sheet materials, complex forms can be built up using careful pattern-making.

Synclastic and Anticlastic Geometries: Pillow or Pringle?

The quintessential anticlastic snack food – Pringles Original.™

The renewed interest in both synclastic and anticlastic geometries continues. Synclastic structure man Ben Morris continues to develop the use and application of low-pressure ETFE (ethylene tetra fluoro ethylene copolymer) foil pillows with his company Vector Foiltec. The firm has recently completed the roof of De Rijke Marsh and Morgan's Kingsdale School in South London with a 5,000-square-metre ETFE envelope that can moderate light transmission through variable pressure in its inflatable skin. Meanwhile, John Zerning's seminal publication on anticlastic forms (*Design Guide To Anticlastic Structures in Plastic*, Polytechnic of Central London, 1976) has found a new reader in young engineer Jessica Brew of Adams Kara Taylor (currently looking into form-finding software and a quoted source on the website of MIT's Kinetic Design Group). The signature anticlastic form of the hyperbolic parabola has recently surfaced atop Richard Rogers Partnership's Antwerp Law Courts, and despite recent product diversification Pringles Original™ continues to be the quintessential anticlastic snack food.

Sound Bubbles

Surveillance railings spotted in Pimlico, London, in 1992.

Sound recordist Tim Davies listening to the landscape.

Hypersonic sound may soon revolutionise the field of electro-acoustics and the electronic production of sound. It uses ultrasonic frequencies (20,000 hertz or greater) that are inaudible to humans. When beamed from an actuator, such frequencies excite the air in their path to produce sound that is audible only when one is positioned within the direct path of the 'beam of sound'. It is the directionality and focus of the sound that is seen as one of its key benefits, as the technology would allow you to walk in and out of tightly controlled sonic zones. American inventor Woody Norris of the American Technology Corporation (ATC) has produced devices that can project a column of sound, and that are being marketed for sound advertisements attached to the vending machines of Japan. ATC claims to have recently produced a single sphere of sound, or a 'sound bubble'. According to Suzanne Kantra Kirschner of *Popular Science* magazine: 'At 30,000 hertz, the sound can travel 150 yards (137 metres) without any distortion or loss of volume.'

Smart Road Humps

A car crossing the Dunlop Transcalm™ in London. The rear light movement demonstrates its smooth passage with minimal disruption.

Recently tested in the City of London are Dunlop's 'intelligent' traffic-calming road humps, called Transcalm. Invented by Graham Heeks, these inflatable barriers adjust their rigidity in accordance with the speed at which you drive over them. The weight of emergency vehicles such as ambulances and fire engines will overcome the barrier to provide an unimpeded route. Transcalm works by incorporating a unique Norgren air valve that controls the rate at which air escapes from the hump when traffic passes over it. The valve can be set to deflate at speeds between 5 and 10 miles per hour.

Ant and Bee

The Antonov AN225 being loaded with a late-ordered Bangkok subway train carriage.

Recently refuelling at Glasgow Prestwick airport in Scotland was the largest commercial freighter in the world – the Antonov AN225. This six-engined plane has a wing span of 88.4 metres (the height of Big Ben) and a lift capacity of 250 tonnes (approximately 90 of Buckminster Fuller's Wichita Dymaxion Houses). Operating at the microscale are the 50-gram micro-aircraft (mechanical bees). The mechanical insects are currently being developed as pilotless reconnaissance craft under the guidance of Dr Ismet Gursul, head of the aerospace sub-group at the University of Bath's department of mechanical engineering, with support from the Ministry of Defence. Dr Gursul says of his current research: 'We are looking for the most efficient way of flying, and the rapid flapping of a flexible wing is one of these, and in this respect we are imitating nature and the flight of insects and birds.'

Computational Fluid Dynamics (CFD)

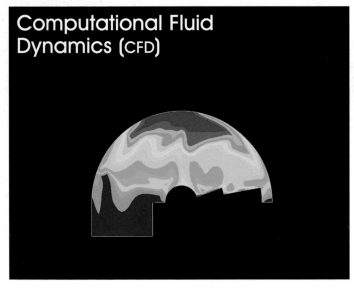

Computational fluid dynamic (CFD) analysis of an igloo.

As part of his ongoing research, Dr Darren Woolf published a paper entitled 'Optimal Environments – CFD Analysis of an Igloo'. Dr Woolf is an environmental engineer working for Arup. He specialises in CFD analyses looking at airflows in buildings, including pollutant distributions and the spread of smoke in a fire. He worked extensively on the heating and ventilation analysis of the recently completed London Coliseum refurbishment. The igloo analysis is predicated on the further technological understanding of our man-made and natural environment. It investigates the indigenous design of the igloo, its form, thermal properties, and complex 'tuneable' heating and ventilation system, and proves that there is much to be learnt from such 'fully optimised enclosures'.

Country Life – Demographics

A recent proposal from the Cairngorm National Park Authority suggests that the park becomes the first in Scotland where farmers receive subsidy, not for agricultural output such as crops, milk and meat production, but for the 'recreational and environmental benefits they offer the public'. A report by David Ross in Scotland's *Herald* newspaper explains that the park authority is to make a call to be designated a region for land management contracts under the Common Agricultural Policy (CAP). The public benefits could modestly include new footpaths and stiles, sacrificial crops for wildlife, and the replanting of native tree species. In a separate report in the same newspaper, by Vicky Collins, we learn that a recent survey in *Country Life* magazine found that 39 per cent of those surveyed said a move to the countryside would lead to 'better quality' sex.

By the Light of the Moon

A Powermoon being used to illuminate roadworks in Germany.

The Helimax Powermoon is a 5.5-metre-diameter helium-filled dirigible light source. Manufactured by Noelle Industrielle of Rheinberg, Germany, this artificial moon has been designed to provide an evenly distributed source of light for road and rail construction, emergency and film lighting. Elevated to 50 metres, the Powermoon can illuminate an area with an 800-metre radius, banishing the harsh shadows of more traditional stand-mounted halogen lamps. Within a radius of 1.5 kilometres, a light level similar to twilight/dusk can be achieved. The Helimax Powermoon contains four 4,000-watt HQI (high-quartz iodide) lamps (approximately a million lumens) despite a relatively low energy consumption. The development of these lights has been made possible through the use of Levapren, a UV-resistant EVM (ethylene and vinyl acetate copolymer) rubber produced by Bayer Polymers, which provides a gas-tight yet relatively transparent skin that has previously been problematic owing to the small size of helium molecules. The 5.5-metre-diameter Helimax Powermoon contains 90 cubic metres of helium. ⌀

AD

A MEMORY OF POSSIBILITIES[1]

One of the many flamboyant covers of Δ illustrated by Adrian George.
This one is called *A Sand Fantasy* and was inspired by the Kuwait Sports Centre
by Kenzo Tange and Frei Otto.

The 1970s was a time of profound change in the life of Δ. Printing methods radically changed to include a lot more colour, the editorial board comprised a healthy generational mix and, by the middle of the decade, the magazine turned to book form. Guest-editor Samantha Hardingham **discovers how the magazine came into its own by publishing everything from ideas on paper to the working details of a sports stadium whilst maintaining a healthy ongoing dialogue between its contributors and readers.**

Ice structures

Last winter, Gianni Pettana iced over an abandoned school in Minneapolis. The ice sheet covering was formed by running water pipes pierced with holes along the top of the building and then turning the water on and letting it flow over the building and set overnight.

Pettana's other projects include a house in Salt Lake City completely covered in clay.

A 2 inch ice shell was built at North Dakota State University; the structure was designed by Wolf Hilbertz and constructed by spraying water over a plastic inflatable. The igloo can withstand and interior temperature of 50 degrees F. without collapsing; it can easily be reinforced, converted and recycled.

The biggest advantage of the structure is that it costs practically nothing: the biggest disadvantage, that its use is restricted to cold climates or winter periods.

D+E

Central Park cake

Haus Rucker Co.'s birthday cake in the form of a 6ft by 24ft scale model of Central Park consisted of such delicacies as in-situ green icing, gooey cake, bread, cream cheese, rolled salami, with pieces of cauliflower to make trees and the paths that wend through the park.

D+E Summer '72

Teeth transmitters

Dr. Irving Glickman, a dental specialist at the University of Boston, has developed special telemetric transmitters which fit inside patients' teeth and relay information about their biting habits.

The doctor wishes to use the transmitters to prove his theory that many gum disorders are caused through excessive biting pressure.

V D I

Oil tank

An intermediate oil storage depot in the Persian Gulf works on the same principle as a diving bell. Designed without a bottom the 'bell' lies submerged in the sea when full of water and slowly rises as the lighter-than-water oil is pumped in at the top. This system of storage has proved cheaper than constructing 100 km long pipelines to take the oil to land-based depots. To transport the tank to its present site the 'bell' was filled with air and towed by tugs; the floating tank is 60 m high.

V D

Typical pages from Cosmorama in the early 1970s show the range of interests that Robin Middleton brought to the readers, and his range of sources, from *Science Journal* to *Architectural and Engineering News*. It is important to note that although seemingly off the wall, all of these items were actually in development or being built somewhere in the world.

The idea: In order to move forward, look back, at the same time as understanding where you are.[2]

This idea is proffered by tutors and professionals as nearing the heart of good design. It was offered to me as a student at the Architectural Association (AA) by my undergraduate tutor Sand Helsel and guest critic Cedric Price whilst attempting to design a theatre on railway tracks. It was exploded spectacularly by diploma tutor John Frazer and his efforts to get his students to compute without computers in the early

1990s (just when we thought we could begin to get our hands on the damn things). And, most recently, the idea has inspired investigations into mobile and wireless technology in relation to the education of an architect, with David Greene at the Research Centre for Experimental Practice at the University of Westminster. Although the word-equation always sounded like the right thing to be doing, I can honestly say that it was difficult to fully understand, not least to think about, how one might apply it. Five factors have emerged in no specific order (or rather been borrowed and chewed) that have helped to bring a degree of clarity, whilst the application remains open for the profession to address.

1 Time is a design tool – it shapes both continuity and change simultaneously.
2 Personal interests in relation to local and global events are not to be underestimated and are rarely unconnected.
3 It is proven that more can be learnt about one's own discipline by looking to alternative areas of expertise, whether the law, medicine or cloud formations.
4 One learns from history, not nostalgia.
5 Everything has a technology.

All of the aforementioned people and points reinforce the need for a) an approach, b) an ability to keep a close eye on the facts, c) to imagine. It is for these reasons that Δ resonates, specifically, those issues published through the late 1960s and up until 1975. It is worth reading them now, whether as a revisit or for the very first time – I can guarantee enjoyment and surprises.

During this particular period, the magazine served as a stunning chronicle of global events, political and economic developments, innovations, grand projects, environmental and social conditions. It was produced monthly under the editorship of Monica Pidgeon who had taken the position in1946 (many magazines having been given over to women to produce during the Second World War). She was assisted by technical editors Theo Crosby, Kenneth Frampton and, then, Robin Middleton who took over from 1964–71. The art department truly came to life in 1969 when Peter Murray joined Adrian George (the man who enjoyed drawing so many of the covers). Murray subsequently succeeded Middleton as technical editor.[3]

Each issue was packed with up-to-the-minute information on anything from art exhibitions to oceanography, alongside in-depth commentary on planning studies, portraits of new built projects and pages and pages of ideas. Cosmorama was invented as a separate section at the beginning of each issue to accommodate the more newsy items. It was for 'commentary on buildings or events throughout the world that impinge on architecture'. The diverse mix of material can be attributed to the three generations that made up the editorial team. Monica Pidgeon had close connections with the postwar Modernists such as Erno Goldfinger, Team 10, the Smithsons and Aldo van Eyck, and was keen to publish them. Theo Crosby was 'into everything – art, architecture, writing. He went to the ICA a lot', remarks Pidgeon, and would then regularly visit the Δ offices with stories of what he had seen. Pidgeon

Drug-induced euphoric proposal for the Paris Biennale, 1969, by the collaborative American group Ant Farm. The parallels with the work of the UK's Archigram and in particular David Greene's L.A.W.U.N project, are striking. The page reads: 'Cities sit as a monument to the past.

Life goes on in greener pastures, and in the midst occurs the oasis, a place where people gather to interact/play/exchange information. The electronic oasis.'

travelled frequently, visiting projects around the world, and everywhere she went she made contacts and engaged them as Δ foreign correspondents. 'People sent things in because they were interested.' Robin Middleton had participated in many of Archigram's activities, had worked at Taylor Woodrow and had a keen interest in the environment in the widest sense. Peter Murray was young blood, a recent graduate of the AA with some experience in publishing as a student having devised the *Clip Kit* magazine as a homage to Archigram.

The Δ magazine was owned by the Standard Catalogue Company (SCC) and the production of issues varied according to the printing techniques employed and economy drive that the owners chose to put in place. The hot-metal plate printing method was used up until the end of the 1960s at which time it changed to the offset lithographic method. The change coincided with an economic downturn at the time, and the SCC was looking for cost-cutting measures. A cheaper printing process and cheaper paper provided an answer. Murray recalls offset litho liberating the process of cutting and pasting, speeding up the whole layout exercise considerably – interestingly the content seemed to particularly flourish at this time.

It was this change in printing technology that allowed Cosmorama to really diversify, and the section became Middleton's own. By now the purpose of the pages was to provide dedicated space to develop idiosyncratic and stimulating ideas. A new section entitled SECTOR was introduced to make more dedicated space for architectural/planning concerns: 'Systems studies, operational research, cybernetics, mathematics, sociology, psychology, epistemology, computer studies … for a start.' This fact alone endures as a unique moment in architectural publishing. It meant that unbuilt and conceptual projects could be viewed and discussed alongside

research and the built. Cosmorama read increasingly like a comic, although the extent and detail of its coverage stood on an equal footing with the more extended features on housing or a newly built university campus. By 1970 there was a printer in Middlesbrough who could print in full colour in one afternoon, and Pidgeon remembers that this is when the fun really began. Cosmorama symbolised a societal awareness (including architects) of a truly pluralistic approach to informing and developing their subject.

We have only recently again caught glimpses of such a multidisciplinary agenda with a new generation being brought up on cheap flights, mobile phones and the World Wide Web at its disposal. These were the things that contributors to Δ in the 1960s and 1970s were dreaming of and drawing. A typical Cosmorama covered on average 30 items over eight pages. Subject matter included: undersea experimental programmes, an advert for *Archigram No 9*, a hoax housing competition by Ant Farm, an article on toy theory, the first home computer, diagrams of a 3-D TV, mass-produced convalescence facilities designed by Mies van der Rohe, a kite competition, a portable operating theatre, a request for ideas for cities, a proposal for comprehensive schools in Germany, expanding clay for raising sagging buildings, a tent/wetsuit for touring motorcyclists, and a spread of projects under the title: 'What are Russian architecture students looking at?' It was a valuable resource, not a magazine to flick through.

David Greene, a regular contributor to Cosmorama, remembers that 'it was always international, inclusive

Architectural Design 12 1972   40p

R BUCKMINSTER FULLER RETROSPECTIVE

The Christmas issue for 1972 displays R Buckminster Fuller appearing to conduct Manhattan.

15

CEDRIC PRICE SUPPLEMENT

INTRODUCTION

For some years AD has been publishing schemes, articles and comments by Cedric Price as one of the prime movers on the radical architecture scene. However, much of his work still remains unpublished and much of the published work requires rethinks and updated commentaries.

To provide a complete picture of his work and ideas, we begin this month a series of supplements which will appear at intervals over the next year. These pages can be taken out of the magazine, filed, recollated, added to or thrown away by the reader; there is space allowed for the reader's own comments and filing code, thus allowing the feature to become a flexible, user-serviced information pool in the best Cedric Price tradition. The presentation is very straight; Price's work lacks strong visual

impact. Unlike most other current radicals (and reactionaries) he is consciously anti-style - sometimes even at the expense of comprehensibility. His drawings have an expressionless aesthetic reminiscent of engineers' working drawings with fine lines and dead pan presentation which, like Le Corbusier's free hand drawings, begin to create a powerful imagery of their own. Standard forms, elevations and perspectives mean little in the terms of Price's work: his plans are kits of parts and circuit diagrams; his details are catalogue specifications. He presents a complete and conscious reversal of current procedure, disposing of the traditional constraints of the pre-electric age and stripping *architecture* down to a *service* with *servicing*. He is perhaps the ultimate/intellectual services engineer dispensing self-pace, self-service, flexible, expendible renewable non-environments - liberating man

from existing rigid structuring while still allowing him to operate within that set-up. Services are toys, things to play with, have fun with. They are all-providing. They are education/information, shelter, transport, baby-sitters, social exchange. They can be controlled by the receiver to suit his needs, receptivity and mood. They are continually available, easily and at any stage.

The *building* could be an existing structure, a clip-on mock tudor facade, an inflatable or a bicycle shed: although that is not to disregard the fact that in some cases a building in the traditional sense may be a valid solution.

His business is problem-solving within the context of user choice, the freedom from environmental constraints and the general improvement of the quality of life; and that's what its all about.

P.M.

FORWARD

To introduce this series I have selected together with Peter Murray a slightly ragged and rum collection which nevertheless establishes the majority of themes for subsequent collections. However, in order to avoid your having to accept such themes, I am merely indexing the schemes under code letters, the definition of which will not be given until the end of the series.

(I have always thought the untitled stamp albums and scrapbooks far more useful).

I realise there is an element of horror comic about all this - if architects' shortfalls were more widely known, then who knows, our individual productivity might be collectively accelerated. I for one would like to know more about local authority housing roofs that, under certain circumstances, can fly.

C.P.

The introductory page for the Cedric Price Supplement series edited by Peter Murray, which appeared in five issues of *AD*. One might argue with Murray that Price's work 'lacks strong visual impact and is anti-style'. Price's draughtsmanship was eminently elegant in its economy of line and use of different media to communicate a point with the skill of the most adept cartoonist.

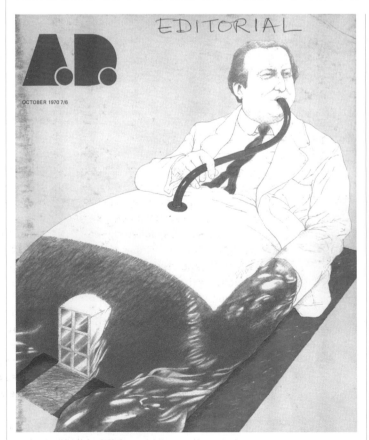

Another illustration by Adrian George of Cedric Price to draw attention to the first issue to include the Cedric Price Supplement. Whether Price is either inflating his own building, dining table or trousers, it is not immediately apparent, but he fittingly rests on a red carpet.

of all technologies, found the unexpected, was focused on architecture as environment in its truest sense. Did you know that the Greek definition of "environment" is "to hit all at once"? The other architectural magazines, like the *Architect's Journal,* were about building: new ceiling systems and damp proof courses.' Greene considers Cedric Price and R Buckminster Fuller to have been the guiding lights.

More, more, more mobile

Both Fuller and Price identified that 'inclusiveness' was central to gaining an understanding of one's environment and that this could be achieved by an increase in mobility: literally on-the-move and via invisible communication networks. 'As people pull up their roots, travelling from summer to winter in hours, the old concept of man as a static temperate, or tropic dweller will change. He will become a man for all seasons.'[5] Fuller's contribution to the environmental debate was covered in a special issue dedicated to the great polymath himself in December 1972. In it he refers to his World Design Science Decade research project (1965–75) conducted with John McHale. This magnanimous project sought not only to compile an 'Inventory of World Resources', but also to propose a method of 'Comprehensive Thinking' that would help to design the necessary network of 'Service Industries', for example world shelter and health facilities. These were not product-orientated industries but invisible support

The first exhibit of the Technical Faculty of the Invisible University curated by David Greene and EXP (Research Centre for Experimental Practice, University of Westminster). A shop window display for Selfridges incorporated interactive devices that tracked the movement of passers-by (Jason Bruges), tracked the sunlight (Chris Leung), changed colour in response to nearby mobile-phone signals (Usman Haque) and imported photographic portraits via a dedicated website and reassembled them on screen (Theo Spyropoulos and Vasili Stroumpakos). The window was supported by the Architecture Foundation as part of Architecture Week, June 2004.

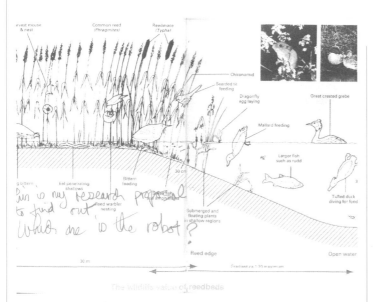

David Greene's research proposal of 2003 continues a lifelong search for nonplace and ambition for the robot to work harder in order for human beings to spend more time working out ways to tune into their environment.

Members of the Technical Faculty of the Invisible University, January 2004. Left to right: Jason Bruges, Usman Haque, Will McLean, Theo Spyropoulos, Vasili Stroumpakos, Chris Leung, David Greene and Pete Silver.

systems that would be 'anticipatorily designed to meet the widest range of [man's] requirements'. Fuller engaged students of architecture on the programme of research because he identified them as the most broadly educated group.

Price was a more regular contributor to $\triangle$. It suited his mode of practice in that items were commissioned and published quickly (within the month), therefore maximising their presentness and limiting the irrelevance of being out of date.[6] Magazine publication also lent itself to Price's anticipatory approach to design; the writing and rewriting down was another way of optimising the scope of possible futures. His supplement series, edited by Peter Murray, appeared in five episodes from October 1970 to January 1972. Devised as a multipage insert (to be collected in the *Clip Kit* fashion), each supplement documented a wide selection of projects, or bits of projects, in words and pictures from the offices of Cedric Price Architects. Additional annotations in Price's own hand were made specifically in light of that particular moment of publishing the work. His economical use of words in the project descriptions, and the story-telling nature of his sketches and factual diagrams, serve in themselves as a manual for architects.

The range of material is again too great to cover here and I can only strongly recommend that readers find them in a library and study them closely. Lasting impressions include the extensive research on Housing

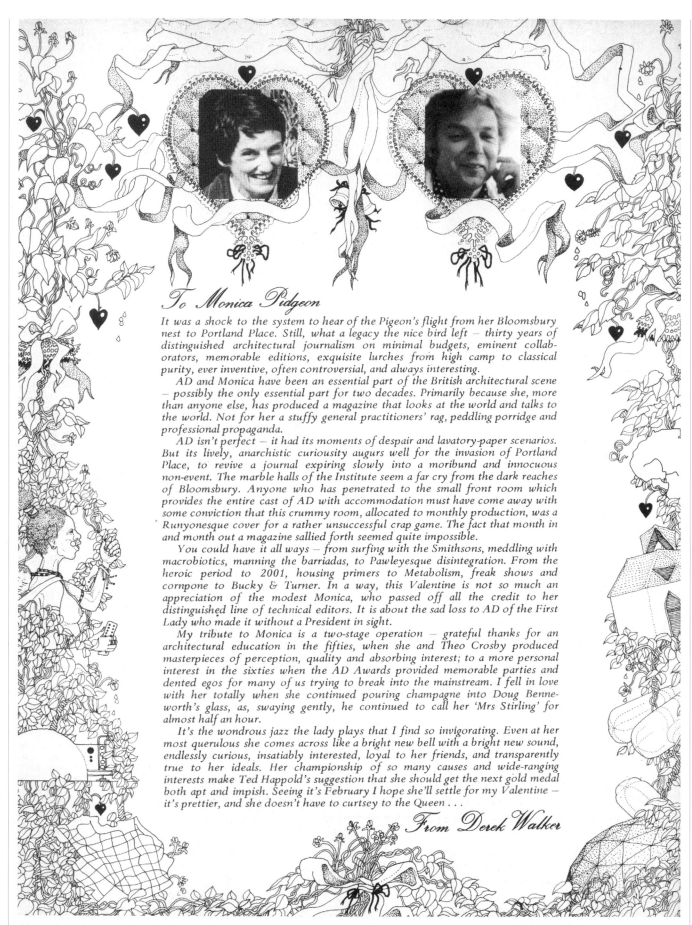

To Monica Pidgeon

It was a shock to the system to hear of the Pigeon's flight from her Bloomsbury nest to Portland Place. Still, what a legacy the nice bird left — thirty years of distinguished architectural journalism on minimal budgets, eminent collaborators, memorable editions, exquisite lurches from high camp to classical purity, ever inventive, often controversial, and always interesting.

AD and Monica have been an essential part of the British architectural scene — possibly the only essential part for two decades. Primarily because she, more than anyone else, has produced a magazine that looks at the world and talks to the world. Not for her a stuffy general practitioners' rag, peddling porridge and professional propaganda.

AD isn't perfect — it had its moments of despair and lavatory-paper scenarios. But its lively, anarchistic curiousity augurs well for the invasion of Portland Place, to revive a journal expiring slowly into a moribund and innocuous non-event. The marble halls of the Institute seem a far cry from the dark reaches of Bloomsbury. Anyone who has penetrated to the small front room which provides the entire cast of AD with accommodation must have come away with some conviction that this crummy room, allocated to monthly production, was a Runyonesque cover for a rather unsuccessful crap game. The fact that month in and month out a magazine sallied forth seemed quite impossible.

You could have it all ways — from surfing with the Smithsons, meddling with macrobiotics, manning the barriadas, to Pawleyesque disintegration. From the heroic period to 2001, housing primers to Metabolism, freak shows and cornpone to Bucky & Turner. In a way, this Valentine is not so much an appreciation of the modest Monica, who passed off all the credit to her distinguished line of technical editors. It is about the sad loss to AD of the First Lady who made it without a President in sight.

My tribute to Monica is a two-stage operation — grateful thanks for an architectural education in the fifties, when she and Theo Crosby produced masterpieces of perception, quality and absorbing interest; to a more personal interest in the sixties when the AD Awards provided memorable parties and dented egos for many of us trying to break into the mainstream. I fell in love with her totally when she continued pouring champagne into Doug Benneworth's glass, as, swaying gently, he continued to call her 'Mrs Stirling' for almost half an hour.

It's the wondrous jazz the lady plays that I find so invigorating. Even at her most querulous she comes across like a bright new bell with a bright new sound, endlessly curious, insatiably interested, loyal to her friends, and transparently true to her ideals. Her championship of so many causes and wide-ranging interests make Ted Happold's suggestion that she should get the next gold medal both apt and impish. Seeing it's February I hope she'll settle for my Valentine — it's prettier, and she doesn't have to curtsey to the Queen . . .

From Derek Walker

A fitting valentine letter from Derek Walker to Monica Pidgeon on the news of her departure from the *AD* editorial team in 1975.

and ThinkGrid, a proposal for an information, resource and programming network to be integrated into the existing education and learning facilities of Oakland County College in Michigan, US. Price comments: 'The legacy of "invisible servicing" is the most valid part of these proposals ... and could well produce new architectural and planning priorities.' The project occurred as a logical progression from his UK-based Potteries Thinkbelt of 1964. In his column '4 Aims for 1970', which formed a prelude to the supplement series, his last note under the subtitle, 'Lift-it' says: 'Familiarise, not only with the weight and dynamic stability of the structure but also its social load.' The word 'priorities' again springs to mind. On a previous occasion Fuller had pointed out the importance of the first two design factors, but Price's extension of the brief to anticipate the consequential impact of a given design on society as a whole inspired the moment. The statement is evidence, too, of the close friendship and correspondence maintained by Price and Fuller.

David Greene's optimistic L.A.W.u.N project, a search for nonplace, existed appropriately through the pages of *Archigram No.9* and then as extracts from his Gardeners Notebook in *Ɒ* (8/70). The acronym stands for Locally Available World Unseen Networks and was launched with a poem entitled 'All watched over by machines of loving grace', written by the self-described 'realist'. Greene imagines a place where man, machine and nature coexist harmoniously and in a mutually beneficial way. 'I can see in my mind a picture of a nomad and within the pocket of his long-haired coat rests a television device ... his own life previously interwoven with his natural environment is now also interwoven with the electronic environment, but both exist together, one does not replace the other ... both together produce a new environment, an electronic aborigine.' Today we can all bump into his 'cowboy international nomad hero' and other characters, such as Bac-Pac man, in the street – they are indeed real. The ubiquitous mobile phone and onset of wireless technology are the enablers, whereas the 'architecture that exists only in reference to time' has been slow to evolve. Or maybe it is that we still have not learnt how to see it yet. The manifestations of that architecture today are not unlike those that existed 35 years ago; caravans and pop festivals. However, developments in robotics and interactive and responsive devices are now informing how we might rethink a time-based architecture.

Today Greene speculates on the effects of the widespread availability of mobile technology in relation to higher education and learning, in particular in a school of architecture. His main concern is what to do about the batteries. In 2004 he founded the Invisible University[7] to assist in these investigations and has appointed its first technical faculty; a number of young architectural practices working in the field of interactive design and research. The connection being made between the two generations, linking thought and electronic practicability, is crucial at this time in creating a new vocabulary of ideas, priorities and values with the capability, not the imagery, that technology has to offer.

No Going Back

The latter part of 1975 marked a turning point in the production of *Ɒ*, its editorial board and a change in the architectural profession's opinion of itself and the way that the practice of architecture has been conducted ever since. The image of the profession up until then had been one of resourcefulness, the belief that technology could find solutions, an understanding that the world had limited resources and a society educated accordingly. Issues published from 1976 onwards reflected a quite different mood: the magazine began to retune its voice to become the megaphone for the imminent arrival of Postmodernism. Of course, it did not happen overnight. Echoes from previous contributors were still being heard intermittently. 'Whatever happened to the systems approach?' by Andrew Rabeneck in May 1976 featured in this article. Rabeneck clearly makes the point that value systems were changing and therefore also the architect's perception of what constituted a design problem, as epitomised in the work of Cedric Price, Walter Segal, Buckminster Fuller and RSM (Research into Site Management which came out of the Nottinghamshire County Architects Dept). Architects began to remove themselves from the responsibilities of determining policy towards broad social issues, and became image-makers rather than imaginers. They remained interested in 'issues' but only as subjective observers.

The role of the architect has never quite recovered from this moment. Haig Beck and Martin Spring became Pidgeon's successors (she edited her last issue in October 1975), and Andreas Papadakis the new owner. Combined with the influence of regular contributor Charles Jencks, classicism and historicism were revived. Pidgeon had initiated the transformation from magazine to book economy at around the time of the budget cuts that had coincided with the changes in printing method. Although almost undetectable at the time, by the late 1970s this had made a significant impact on the structure, content and design of the publication, driven primarily by the difference between production schedules (exactly one month and approximately 12 months respectively) and pricing.

Italo Calvino wrote 30 years ago: 'There is less uncertainty in the things that are only meant to last for a particular amount of time.'[8] Will Alsop said last year: 'When there are no ideas in magazines, it encourages young architects to think that they have to build.' There is a legacy in the issues of *Ɒ* discussed here that will remain for as long as it is useful to print ideas. *Ɒ*

Notes
1 Will Alsop's description of the exhibition entitled 'Out of the Box' at the Canadian Centre for Architecture (CCA) in 2003/4, which displayed projects by four key figures from the 1970s – James Stirling, Aldo Rossi, Cedric Price and Gordon Matta-Clark – all of whom have work held in the archives of the CCA.
2 Or, as John McHale so eloquently put it (*Ɒ*, '2000+', Vol 37, February 1967): 'The future of the past is in the future. The future of the present is in the past. The future of the future is in the present.'
3 Detailed accounts of life on the magazine from members of the editorial team appear in *Ɒ*, Vol 70, No 5, October 2000, p 98 – 'Being There', by Haig Beck; *Ɒ*, Vol 70, No 6, December 2000, p 98 – 'A Critical Contribution', by Charles Jencks; and *Ɒ*, Vol 71, No 2, April 2001, p 96 – 'Being Remembered 1941–75', by Monica Pidgeon.
4 'Clip Kit was a kit of pages that was produced in batches over a six-month period and sent off to subscribers who slipped them into a plastic clip.' – Peter Murray
5 R Buckminster Fuller with Jerome Agel and Quentin Fiore, *I Seem to be a Verb*, Bantam Books (New York), 1970.
6 Three books were published on Cedric Price's work during his lifetime: *Cedric Price Works II* (Architectural Association, 1984), republished as *Cedric Price: The Square Book* (Wiley-Academy, 2003); *Cedric Price Opera* (ed Samantha Hardingham, Wiley-Academy, 2003); and *RE:CP* (by Cedric Price, ed Hans Ulrich Obrist, Birkhauser Verlag AG, August 2003).
7 The first meeting of the Technical Faculty of the Invisible University was held on 18 March 2004. Speakers were selected by David Greene, Will McLean and Pete Silver with EXP and included: Jason Bruges, Chris Leung, Usman Haque, Theo Spyropoulos, Vasili Stroumpakos and Jon Goodbun.
8 Italo Calvino, *Invisible Cities*, Vintage, 1997. First published in Italy by Giulio Einaudi editore, 1972.

OUT-IN-THE-OPEN

UNIVERSITY

There is a tradition of maps as inserts in magazines to assemble particular points of interest that are relevant and useful to the moment. ⧋ was, and is, no exception to this, and as a student research assistant in the Research Centre for Experimental Practice (EXP) at the University of Westminster, **Nick Lister** has generated a group of maps for the current phase of David Greene and EXP's research project L.A.W.U.N – the Invisible University. The original project imagined a serviced landscape, and was presented in the pages of ⧋ between 1968 and 1970. Today, the research speculates on the relationship between mobile and wire-free technology and the architecture school in determining the future education of an architect. These maps present three types of serviced landscapes present in the UK in 2004: regional parkland ecologies, locations and access between places of higher education, and the national mobile communications network. These typologies relate the first stage of a comparative study that will be used to develop the brief of the Invisible University.

National Parks in the UK

1 Brecon Beacons
134,700ha
47,957ha common land
A mountainous region with a number of forests and lakes, the park also has an area dotted with waterfalls and gorges along its southern rim. 58,451ha is given over to open country while most of the rest is occupied by agriculture, the area's major industry.

2 Dartmoor
95,600ha
37,028ha common land
47 per cent of the park is wild moorland. The landscape rises in parts to granite tors and falls to wooded river valleys. The whole is edged with small fields. Wildlife includes buzzards and dormice, lichens and mosses. The Ministry of Defence (MoD) occupies 14 per cent of the park, while the rest finds its major industry in the rough grazing of stock.

3 Exmoor
69,300ha
Beyond the cliffy shoreline of Exmoor are broadleaf woodland and a predominant central plateau of grass moorland. This is surrounded by heather-covered hills that catch Atlantic clouds and feed numerous rivers. The area is largely dependent on tourism and agriculture, which occupies 39,371ha. The park has a large variety of wildlife including the Exmoor pony and birds of prey.

4 Lake District
229,200ha
16,460ha common land
A cold and wet area characterised by its mountains, lakes and heather-, grass- and bracken-covered open fell. Major settlements like Keswick house most of the resident population, as well as services for the park's 12 million annual visitors, and are the area's industrial base. Wildlife includes red squirrels and ravens, as well as fish in the rivers and lakes, and grazing sheep.

5 Northumberland
104,900ha
150ha common land
The park has three parts. To the north are the moors and grassland of the Cheviot Hills; the centre and west contain three major river valleys; and in the south is the Whin Sill ridge, which includes Hadrian's Wall. One notable feature is the MoD's Otterburn Training Area, which occupies 22.6 per cent of the park; 18.9 per cent is occupied by the Forestry Commission, which alongside agriculture gives the area its major industry. Grouse are common in the park.

6 North York Moors
143,600ha
23,380ha common land
The park has 48km of cliffed and rocky coastline, tabular hills along its south edge, woodland to the southeast, and around 57,000ha of farmland and villages along the valleys and coast. Tourism is the major industry, with farming and forestry in support. Deer, fallow deer, grouse, otters and merlin, as well as many other birds, can be found in the park.

7 Peak District
143,800ha
Attracting 22 million visitors each year, the Peak District is the second most visited national park in the world. Between the wild millstone peak to the north and the rolling limestone peak to the south are the Derwent and Wye valleys, home to the largest settlements and a number of stately homes. Although tourism forms the major industry, 13.5 per cent of the land is used by water companies. There is also manufacturing, farming and mineral extraction.

8 Pembrokeshire Coast
58,400ha
4,593ha common land
The park is primarily spread along 272km of rugged cliffs and islands of the Welsh coastline, with tree-lined estuaries and moorland also featuring. 85.7 per cent of the land is privately occupied, and 38,836ha is used for agriculture, which with tourism is the area's major industry. Seals and seabirds are the main wildlife.

9 Snowdonia
214,200ha
22,979ha common land
A glacier-formed landscape of U-shaped valleys, cliff faces and mountain lakes, Snowdonia contains the highest peak in England and Wales. Tourism and agriculture are the major industries. Most of the land is privately farmed and owned, although 15.8 per cent is occupied by the Forestry Commission. Birds of prey, otters, moths, choughs and beetles feature among the area's wildlife.

10 Yorkshire Dales
176,900ha
49,300ha common land
52 per cent of this upland limestone country is heather-covered fell, with most of the rest being hay meadows and walled fields. Pastoral valleys, waterfalls and caves also feature. 96.1 per cent of the park's land is privately owned. The area was formerly heavily reliant on coal mining, but farming is now the major industry. Wildlife includes sheep and cattle, grouse and buzzards.

11 The Broads
30,300ha
The park is centred around 63 broads (shallow lakes) that are connected by six rivers. Eighteen of the broads, making up 400ha of open water, are open to navigation. The land around the waterways is often used for grazing cattle, though recreation is the major industry here. Waterfowl, butterflies, dragonflies as well as other wetland insects form most of the park's wildlife.

12 Cairngorms
380,000ha
This mountainous region of the Cairngorms is one of the highest areas in the UK. There are forests around its foothills, and many rivers, lochs and marshes. 74 per cent of the land is farmland, though tourism (including three skiing resorts) accounts for 41 per cent of the area's industry, with support from whisky production, salmon fishing and private hunting. Grouse and deer, as well as red squirrels, badgers and wildcats, are the most notable of the wildlife.

13 Loch Lomond and the Trossachs
186,500ha
The rolling lowlands of the park's southern parts give way to high mountains in the north, with many lochs, rivers, forests and woodlands throughout. Tourism is the most significant part of the economy, and wildlife includes wild cats, red squirrels, capercailzie, osprey, salmon and trout.

Common Land
Common land is land owned by one party to which other parties are granted 'rights of common'. These rights may include rights of access, grazing animals, gathering plants for livestock bedding or digging peat. Although rights of common are specific to individual land units, the provisions of Countryside and Rights of Way Act 2000 will soon give the public the right of access on foot to nearly all 545,000ha registered common land in England and Wales.

Map of National Parks in the UK

■ National Park ── Mainline Railways
■ Total green belt and metropolitan open land in London (49,946ha)

0km   50   100   200

University Campuses in the UK

UoL denotes a college of the University of London
UoW denotes a college of the University of Wales

1 University of Aberdeen
a. Old Aberdeen Campus, urban/suburban
b. Foresterhill Campus, suburban/urban
c. Hilton Campus, suburban/urban
d. Marischal College, urban

2 University of Abertay Dundee
University of Abertay, urban

3 Anglia Polytechnic University
a. Chelmsford, suburban; architecture course (School of Design and Communication Systems, Department of the Built Environment)
b. Cambridge, suburban

4 Aston University
Aston, urban

5 University of Bath
a. Oakfield Campus, urban
b. University of Bath, rural/suburban; architecture course (Faculty of Engineering and Design, Architecture and Civil Engineering)

6 Birkbeck College, UoL
Birkbeck, urban

7 University of Birmingham
a. Edgbaston Campus, suburban
b. Selly Oak Campus, suburban
c. Westhill, suburban

8 Bolton Institute
a. Deane Campus, suburban
b. Chadwick Campus, suburban

9 Bournemouth University
a. Talbot Campus, suburban
b. Lansdowne Campus, urban/suburban

10 University of Bradford
a. Main Campus, urban
b. School of Management, suburban
c. Laisteridge Lane, urban
d. School of Health Studies, urban

11 University of Brighton
a. Eastbourne, suburban
b. Falmer, rural
c. Grand Parade, urban
d. Moulsecoomb, urban; architecture course (Faculty of Arts and Architecture, School of Architecture and Design)

12 University of Bristol
a. University Precinct, urban/suburban
b. Langford, rural

13 Brunel University
a. Uxbridge Campus, suburban
b. Runnymede Campus, rural/suburban
c. Osterley Campus, suburban
d. Twickenham Campus, suburban

14 University of Buckingham
a. Hunter Street Precinct, suburban/rural
b. Chandos Road, suburban/rural
c. Verney Park, suburban/rural

15 University of Cambridge
a. Old Schools, urban
b. Sidgwick, suburban
c. Silver Street/Mill Lane, urban
d. New Museums, urban
e. Downing, urban
f. Old Addenbrooke's, urban; architecture course (Department of Architecture)
g. West Cambridge, rural
h. Mathematical Sciences, suburban

16 Cardiff University
a. Cathays Park Campus, suburban/urban; architecture course (Welsh School of Architecture)
b. Heath Park Campus, suburban

17 University of Central England in Birmingham
a. Perry Barr, suburban; architecture course (Faculty of the Built Environment, School of Architecture and Landscape)
b. Gosta Green, urban
c. Vittoria Street, urban/suburban
d. Margaret Street, urban/suburban
e. Conservatoire, urban
f. Westbourne Campus, suburban
g. Bournville Campus, suburban
h. Millennium Point, urban

18 University of Central Lancashire
a. Preston City Centre, urban
b. Cumbria Campus, rural

19 University of Derby
a. Kedleston Road Campus, suburban
b. Mickleover Campus, suburban/rural
c. Britannia Mill Campus, suburban/rural
d. Buxton Campus, suburban/rural

20 City University
a. Northampton Square site, urban
b. Bath Street, urban
c. The City, urban

d. West Smithfield, urban
e. Holborn, urban
f. Whitechapel, urban

21 Courtauld Institute of Art, UoL
Somerset House, urban

22 Coventry University
Coventry, urban

23 Cranfield University
a. Cranfield, rural
b. Silsoe, rural
c. Shrivenham, rural/suburban

24 De Montfort University
a. City Campus, urban; architecture course (Faculty of Art and Design)
b. Charles Frear, suburban
c. Lansdowne Campus, suburban
d. Polhill Campus, suburban

25 University of Dundee
a. Main Campus, urban; architecture course (Faculty of Duncan of Jordanstone College, School of Architecture)
b. Gardyne, suburban
c. Ninewells, suburban
d. Kirkcaldy, suburban

26 University of Durham
a. University of Durham, urban
b. Queen's Campus, suburban

27 University of East Anglia
University of East Anglia, suburban/rural

28 University of East London
a. Stratford, suburban
b. Docklands, suburban; architecture course (School of Architecture and the Visual Arts)
c. Barking, suburban

29 University of Edinburgh
a. Central Campus, urban; architecture course (School of Arts, Culture and Environment, Department of Architecture)
b. Kings Buildings, urban

30 University of Essex
a. Colchester Campus, rural
b. East 15, suburban
c. Southend, urban

31 University of Exeter
a. Streatham Campus, urban/suburban
b. St Luke's Campus, urban

c. Tremough, rural

32 University of Glamorgan
a. Main Campus, rural
b. Glyntaf Site, rural

33 University of Glasgow
a. Gilmorehill Campus and Glasgow buildings, urban/suburban
b. Crichton Campus, rural

34 Glasgow Caledonian University
City Campus, urban

35 Goldsmiths College, UoL
Goldsmiths, suburban

36 University of Gloucestershire
a. Francis Close Hall, urban/suburban
b. Hardwick Campus, urban/suburban
c. Park Campus, urban/suburban
d. Pittville Campus, suburban
e. Oxtalls Campus, suburban

37 University of Greenwich
a. Avery Hill, suburban; architecture course (School of Architecture and Construction, Department of Design)
b. Maritime Greenwich, suburban
c. Kings Hill Institute, suburban
d. Medway, suburban/rural

38 Heriot-Watt University
a. Edinburgh Campus, rural
b. Scottish Borders Campus, rural

39 University of Hertfordshire
a. St Albans, urban
b. De Havilland Campus, suburban
c. Fielder Centre, suburban
d. College Lane Campus, suburban
e. Bayfordbury Field Station and Observatory, rural

40 University of Huddersfield
Queensgate Campus, urban; architecture course (School of Design Technology)

41 University of Hull
a. Hull Campus, suburban
b. Scarborough Campus, suburban

42 Imperial College London, UoL
a. Charing Cross, urban/suburban
b. The Hammersmith, urban/suburban
c. Royal Brompton Campus, urban
d. South Kensington Campus, urban
e. St Mary's, urban
f. Silwood Campus, rural
g. Wye Campus, rural

Map of University Campuses in the UK

- 150a Campus with architecture course
- 151c Campus with RIBA-validated architecture course

— Mainline railways

0km 50 100 200

43 Institute of Education, UoL
Institute of Education, urban

44 Keele University
Keele, rural

45 University of Kent
a. Canterbury, suburban/rural
b. Brussels School of International Studies, suburban/rural
c. Bridge Wardens' College, suburban
d. Horsted Campus, suburban
e. The University Centre at Tonbridge, suburban

46 King's College London, UoL
a. Strand Campus, urban
b. Guy's Campus, urban
c. St Thomas' Campus, urban
d. Waterloo Campus, urban
e. Denmark Hill, urban/suburban
f. Hampstead Campus, suburban
g. Half Moon Lane, suburban
h. Wellington Hall, urban

47 Kingston University
a. Kingston Hill, suburban
b. Knights Park, suburban; architecture course (Faculty of Art, Design and Music, School of Architecture and Landscape)
c. Penrhyn Road, suburban/urban
d. Roehampton Vale, suburban

48 University of Lancaster
University of Lancaster, rural

49 University of Leeds
a. University of Leeds, urban
b. Bretton Hall, rural
c. Wakefield Campus, suburban/rural

50 Leeds Metropolitan University
a. City Campus, urban; architecture course (Faculty of Arts and Society, the Leeds School of Architecture, Landscape and Design)
b. Headingley Campus, suburban
c. Harrogate Campus, suburban

51 University of Leicester
a. University of Leicester, urban
b. Robert Kilpatrick Clinical Services, urban
c. Vaughan College, urban

52 University of Lincoln
a. Hull Campus, urban
b. Anlaby Road Campus, urban
c. Cathedral Campuses, urban
d. Brayford Campus, suburban; architecture course (Faculty of Art, Architecture and Design, Lincoln School of Architecture)
e. Riseholme Campus, rural

53 University of Liverpool
University of Liverpool, urban; architecture course (Faculty of Social and Environmental Studies, School of Architecture and Building Engineering)

54 Liverpool John Moores University
a. City Campus, urban
b. Mount Pleasant Campus, urban; architecture course (Faculty of Media, Arts and Social Science)
c. I M Marsh Campus, suburban

55 London Business School, UoL
London Business School, urban

56 London Metropolitan University
a. London City, urban
b. London North, suburban/urban; architecture course (Department of Architecture and Spatial Design)

57 London School of Economics and Political Science
London School of Economics and Political Science, urban

58 London School of Hygiene and Tropical Medicine, UoL
London School of Hygiene and Tropical Medicine, urban

59 London South Bank University
a. Southwark Campus, urban/suburban; architecture course (Faculty of Engineering, Science and the Built Environment, Department of Architecture and Design)
b. Essex Campus, suburban
c. East London Campus, suburban

60 Loughborough University
a. Loughborough University, suburban
b. Loughborough University School of Art and Design, urban

61 University of Luton
a. Park Square Campus, urban
b. Putteridge Bury Campus, rural

62 University of Manchester
University of Manchester, urban; architecture course (Faculty of Arts, the Manchester School of Architecture)

63 University of Manchester Institute of Science and Technology (UMSIT) UMSIT, urban

64 Manchester Metropolitan University
a. All Saints, urban
b. Aytoun, urban
c. Elizabeth Gaskell, urban
d. Hollings, urban
e. Didsbury, urban/suburban
f. Crewe, suburban/rural
g. Alsager, rural/suburban

65 Middlesex University
a. Cat Hill Campus, suburban; architecture course (School of Arts)
b. Enfield Campus, suburban
c. Hendon Campus, suburban
d. Tottenham Campus, suburban
e. Trent Park Campus, rural
f. Archway and Hospitals Campus, suburban

66 Napier University
a. Merchiston, suburban
b. Craighouse, suburban
c. Sighthill, suburban
d. Morningside, suburban
e. Craiglockhart, suburban
f. Comely bank, suburban
g. Canaan lane, suburban
h. Redwood, suburban
i. Marchmont, suburban

67 University of Newcastle
University of Newcastle Upon Tyne, urban; architecture course (Faculty of Humanities and Social Sciences, School of Architecture, Planning and Landscape)

68 North East Wales Institute of Higher Education
a. Regent Street Campus, suburban/rural
b. Plas Coch, suburban/rural

69 University of Northumbria at Newcastle
a. Newcastle City Campus, urban; architecture course (School of the Built Environment)
b. Coach Lane Campus, rural
c. University Campus, Carlisle, urban/suburban

70 University of Nottingham
a. Jubilee Campus, suburban
b. Medical School, suburban
c. University Park, suburban; architecture course (Faculty of Law and Social Sciences, School of Built Environment)
d. Sutton Bonington, rural

71 Nottingham Trent University
a. City Campus, urban
b. Brackenhurst Campus, rural
c. Clifton Campus, suburban/rural

72 Open University
a. Scotland Centre, urban
b. North Centre, suburban/urban
c. Yorkshire Centre, urban
d. North West Centre, suburban
e. Wales Centre, suburban/urban
f. West Midlands Centre, suburban
g. East Midlands Centre, suburban/urban
h. East of England Centre, suburban
i. South West Centre, urban
j. South Centre, rural
k. London Centre, urban
l. South East Centre, rural/suburban

73 University of Oxford
a. Oxford City Centre, urban
b. John Radcliffe Hospital Site, suburban

74 Oxford Brookes University
a. Headington Campus, suburban; architecture course (School of the Built Environment, Department of Architecture)
b. Harcourt Hill, suburban/rural
c. Wheatley Campus, rural

75 University of Paisley
a. Paisley Campus, suburban
b. University Campus, Ayr, suburban
c. Crichton University Campus, Dumfries, rural

76 University of Plymouth
a. Plymouth Campus, urban; architecture course (Faculty of Arts, School of Architecture and Design)
b. Exeter Campus, suburban
c. Exmouth Campus, urban
d. Seale-Hayne Campus, suburban/rural
e. Pool Campus, suburban/rural
f. Taunton Campus, suburban

77 University of Portsmouth
a. University Quarter, urban; architecture course (Faculty of the Environment, School of Architecture)
b. Langstone Campus, suburban

78 University of Reading
a. Whiteknights Campus, suburban
b. London Road Campus, suburban
c. Bulmershe Campus, suburban/rural

79 Queen Margaret University College
a. Clerwood, suburban
b. Gateway, urban/suburban
c. Leith, suburban

80 Queen Mary, University of London, UoL
a. Mile End Campus, suburban
b. Whitechapel Campus, suburban
c. West Smithfield Campus, urban
d. Charterhouse Square Campus, urban

81 Queen's University of Belfast
a. Armagh Campus, urban; architecture course (Faculty of Engineering, School of Architecture)
b. Queen's University of Belfast, suburban

82 The Robert Gordon University
a. City Centre Campus, urban
b. Garthdee Campus, suburban/rural; architecture course (Scott Sutherland School)

83 Roehampton University
a. Roehampton Lane Campus, suburban
b. Whitelands College, suburban

84 Royal Academy of Music
Royal Academy of Music, urban

85 Royal College of Art
Royal College of Art, urban; architecture course (Department of Architecture and Interiors)

86 Royal College of Music
Royal College of Music, urban

87 Royal Holloway, University of London, UoL
Royal Holloway, rural/suburban

88 The Royal Veterinary College, UoL
a. Camden Town Campus, urban
b. Hawkshead Campus, rural

89 Royal Welsh College of Music and Drama
Royal Welsh College of Music and Drama, suburban/urban

90 University of Salford
a. University of Salford, suburban
b. Peel House, suburban

91 School of Oriental and African Studies, UoL
a. Russell Square, urban
b. Vernon Square, urban

92 University of Sheffield
University of Sheffield, urban/suburban; architecture course (Faculty of Architectural Studies, School of Architecture)

93 Sheffield Hallam University
a. City Campus, urban; architecture course (School of Environment and Development)
b. Collegiate Crescent, suburban/urban
c. Psalter Lane, suburban

94 University of Southampton
a. Avenue Campus, suburban
b. Boldrewood Campus, suburban
c. Highfield Campus, suburban
d. Southampton General Hospital, suburban
e. Southampton Oceanography Centre, urban/suburban
f. New College, urban/suburban
g. Winchester School of Art, urban/suburban

95 University of St Andrews
University of St Andrews, urban/suburban

96 St George's Hospital Medical School, UoL
St George's Hospital, suburban

97 Staffordshire University
a. Stoke Campus, urban/suburban
b. Stafford Campus, rural
c. Lichfield Campus, rural/suburban

98 University of Stirling
a. University of Stirling, suburban/rural
b. Highland Campus, suburban/rural
c. Western Isles Campus, suburban

99 University of Strathclyde
a. Jordanhill Campus, suburban
b. John Anderson Campus, urban; architecture course (Faculty of Engineering, Department

of Architecture and Building Science)

100 University of Sunderland
a. The City Campus, suburban
b. Sir Tom Cowie Campus, urban/suburban

101 University of Surrey
University of Surrey, suburban

102 University of Sussex
University of Sussex, rural

103 Swansea Institute of Higher Education
a. Mount Pleasant Campus, urban
b. Townhill Campus, suburban

104 University of Teesside
University of Teesside, urban

105 Thames Valley University
a. Ealing Campus, suburban
b. Slough Campus, urban

106 Trinity College
Trinity College, rural

107 University of Ulster
a. Belfast, suburban; architecture course (Faculty of Arts, School of Art and Design)
b. Jordanstown, suburban
c. Coleraine, urban
d. Magee, urban

108 University of the Arts London
a. Camberwell College of Arts, suburban
b. Central Saint Martins College of Art and Design, urban
c. Chelsea College of Art and Design, urban
d. London College of Communication, suburban/urban
e. London College of Fashion, Barrett Street, urban
f. London College of Fashion, John Prince's Street, urban
g. London College of Fashion, Davies Street, urban
h. London College of Fashion, Barbican, urban
i. London College of Fashion, Curtain Road, urban
j. London College of Fashion, Mare Street, suburban

109 University College London, UoL
a. Gower Street Site, urban; architecture course (The Bartlett, Faculty of the Built Environment, the Bartlett School of Architecture)
b. St Pancras Hospital, urban
c. Old Street Site, urban

110 University of Wales Institute, Cardiff, UoW
a. Colchester Avenue Campus, suburban
b. Cyncoed Campus, suburban
c. Howard Gardens Campus, suburban/urban
d. Llandaff Campus, suburban

111 University of Wales, Aberystwyth, UoW
University of Wales, Aberystwyth, rural

112 University of Wales, Bangor, UoW
University of Wales, Bangor, urban

113 University of Wales, Lampeter, UoW
University of Wales, Lampeter, suburban/rural

114 University of Wales, Newport, UoW
a. Allt-yr-yn Campus, urban/suburban
b. Caerleon Campus, suburban/rural

115 University of Wales, Swansea, UoW
University of Wales, Swansea, suburban

116 University of Warwick
a. Central Campus, suburban/rural
b. Gibbet Hill Campus, suburban/rural
c. Westwood Campus, suburban/rural

117 University of the West of England, Bristol
a. Bower Ashton, suburban/rural
b. Frenchay, rural/suburban; architecture course (Faculty of the Built Environment)
c. Glenside, suburban
d. St Matthias, suburban

118 University of Westminster
a. Regent Street Campus, urban
b. Cavendish Campus, urban; architecture course (School of Architecture and the Built Environment, Department of Architecture)
c. Marylebone Campus, urban
d. Harrow Campus, suburban/rural
e. Euston Campus, urban

119 University of Wolverhampton
a. City Campus, urban/suburban
b. Compton Park Campus, suburban
c. Telford Campus, suburban
d. Walsall Campus, suburban

120 University of York
Heslington, suburban/rural

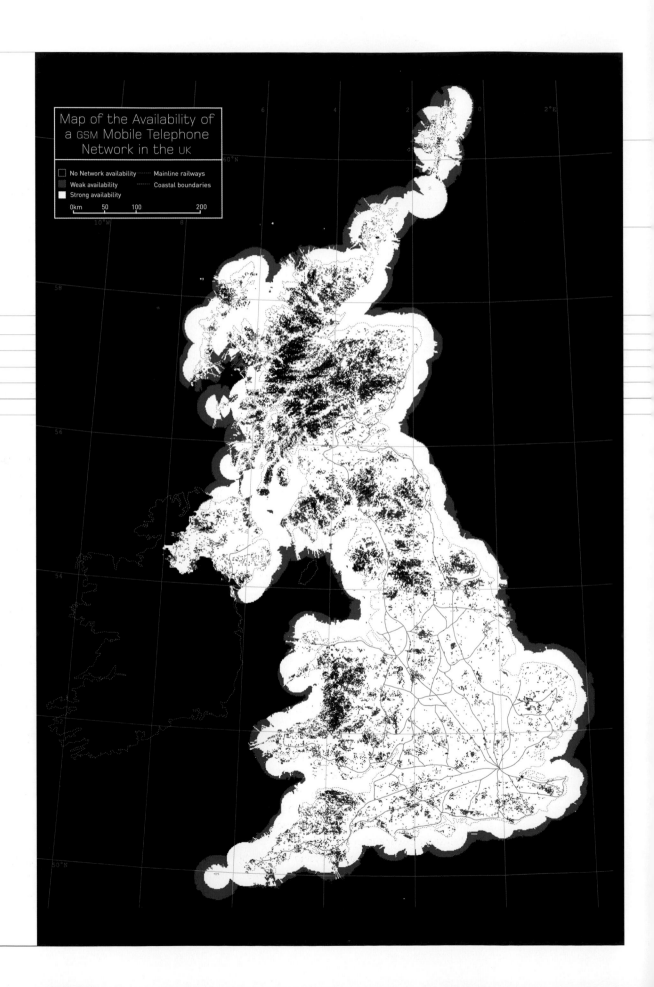

Map of the Availability of a GSM Mobile Telephone Network in the UK

☐ No Network availability ····· Mainline railways
■ Weak availability ····· Coastal boundaries
■ Strong availability

0km   50   100   200

CELLULAR TELEPHONE NETWORKS

Mobile telephones operate across radio communications networks at specially dedicated frequency ranges (around 900MHz and 1800MHz in the UK). Radio signals are transmitted from the phone to the nearest 'base station' (commonly thought of as masts) and from the base station to the phone at slightly different frequencies. The base stations are attached to the main telephone network by either telephone cables or by high-frequency transmissions between antennas.

The area to which radio coverage is offered by each base station is called a cell, hence the 'cellular network'. The base stations are connected by switching centres that track calls and transfer them across the network as the caller moves. To offer total coverage, the ideal network is a mesh of hexagonal cells.

Although base stations currently have a maximum range of 35 kilometres (with practical coverage within 10 kilometres), the size of each cell may be limited by a number of factors. The local terrain may mean that buildings, trees and other objects impede the signal. If the network is operating at a high frequency band, the area of coverage offered by one cell is reduced. Capacity for calls is also a limiting factor on the size of cells; for this reason the spacing of base stations in towns is likely to be between 0.2 kilometres and 0.5 kilometres, while in the countryside it is likely to be between 2 kilometres and 5 kilometres.

Because of the limited range of frequencies available to network operators, frequencies have to be reused across the network to accommodate all the users. To avoid interference from similar frequencies, cells are grouped in repeating clusters where each cell is allocated a different frequency range. In practical terms each cell is able to support about 30 calls at the same time; thus in order to increase network capacity the reuse of frequencies has to occur over a smaller area, which means that smaller cells and more base stations are required. Currently there are around 35,000 base stations in the UK.

There are three types of cell, classified by size. The largest are macrocells; the antennas for these are mounted on masts or high buildings, they operate at (comparatively) high power and usually cover a wide area. Macrocells account for most of the coverage of cellular networks. Microcells are used primarily to offer extra network capacity to areas with many users; the antennas are small and mounted at street level on buildings, lamp posts and street furniture, often being disguised as building features. The typical coverage of a microcell is between 0.3 kilometres and 1 kilometre. Picocells are the smallest cells, providing extra, localised coverage on a small scale. They are most often used to provide extra coverage inside buildings or extra capacity in areas of very high network use.

Currently there are around 40 million people who use mobile phones in the UK, which equates to about 60 per cent of the total population. Most of these people use the Global System for Mobile Communications, or Groupe Speciale Mobile (GSM) to attach wirelessly to the global telecommunications network. GSM is best known as the system that is used by second-generation mobile telephones.

THINGS TO CONSIDER NEXT

Global Parks
Locations of international campuses linked to UK universities and those of the UK-based campuses linked to international universities.
Use of campuses out of term time – is there an out-of-term time?
Student travel distances between home/type of home (shared, parents, tent etc) and chosen university/place of learning – national/international.
Wireless networks – international hotspots. ◬

Below Matter-of-fact Modernism, bicycles and Volkswagen beetles. Van Klingeren's multipurpose activity centre at Dronten, the Netherlands, in 1969.

THE AGORA AT DRONTEN

Below Matter-of-fact Modernism, bicycles and Volkswagen beetles. Van Klingeren's multipurpose activity centre at Dronten, the Netherlands, in 1969.

Rarely has a single building represented and fostered so completely the notion of public realm by serving its public first before drawing attention to itself. **James Madge** finds the Agora at Dronten, in the Netherlands, one such triumph. Through analysing Martin Pawley's review of the building in $\triangle$ in 1969, Madge wonders if it could only have been built in the Netherlands and whether we in the UK will ever learn.

In its July 1969 issue, $\triangle$ devoted five pages to the De Meerpaal multipurpose centre at Dronten, which had been completed some two years previously to the design of architect/engineer F van Klingeren. This was Van Klingeren's first opportunity to develop the solution of a building type for which there was widespread enthusiasm in the Netherlands during the 1960s and into the 1970s. Visual coverage of the centre stressed the variety of sporting, recreational and cultural activities the building was able to accommodate, and its relaxed, open-ended and democratic response to the needs of its users. However, the text, written by Martin Pawley, called into question the validity not only of this, but of all similarly motivated projects the objective of which Pawley describes as a 'grass-roots-reactivated public realm'.

Recognising, on the one hand, that the so-called Agora at Dronten exemplifies almost to perfection the aspirations implicit in buildings of this type, Pawley has felt himself obliged, nevertheless, to pour very cold water over those aspirations and those buildings, assuring his readers that 'by the year 2000 it [the Agora] will either have suffered a complete change of use, or have been demolished in the course of redevelopment', and that 'I consider it to be already out of date.' His arguments are summarised under the following headings: (a) Increased leisure time? You must be joking, (b) Media privatise, they do not publicise, (c) Life is catching up with art, and (d) The public realm is not safe any more. Under each he wants to show that the ills of Western capitalist culture lie beyond the reach of architectural good intentions.

The first argument is founded in an economic view by which those who are not engaged in productive manufacture at globally competitive rates of pay must sooner or later succumb to mass unemployment 'or revolutionary paralysis'; that increased moonlighting, merely to retain his present economic position, will be the fate of the European worker, and that projections of an automated, work-free future are spurious. In the Western Europe of the 21st century, where almost the only thing successfully manufactured is economic reality itself, the impression of greater leisure, supported by a massive leisure industry, must seem, for many people (including, one would suspect, those who live at Dronten) convincing enough: if there is a meaningful distinction between mass unemployment and extended leisure, then capital has evidently found ways to disguise it. Productive labour can be purchased wherever it is, for the time being, cheapest, but it is upon a perpetually expanding access to the means of consumption that modern economies are now, critically, seen to depend.

That 'the media' (Pawley acknowledges his debt to the ideas of Marshall McLuhan) may be seen as contributory – if not decisive – in the dissolution of the public realm, might be more self-evident in 2004 than it was in 1969; since Pawley wrote, the Internet and the mobile phone might be said to have effectively despatialised even the social realm. Curiously, on the other hand, as the nuclear family has lost its universal grip on individual behaviour, the same lapse of time has seen the emergence of numerous activities not related to the home. Cinema attendance, patronage of clubs and fitness facilities, live soccer in bars and museum admissions, not to mention tourism, have all been on the increase. Pawley's more general observation that 'Parker Morris space standards, central heating and piped water, by simply keeping people at home' have tended to promote the decline of public life amongst the lower orders may, indeed, be correct, but it is hardly, in itself, a cause for regret if such public life had been no more than a consequence of inadequate living standards. The assertive presence of those classes in what must today pass for 'public space' is demonstration, if of nothing else, of the extent to which the repressive paternalism of early postwar welfare is now a thing of the past.

In suggesting that 'Life is catching up with art', Pawley is placing Dronten's Agora in the same bracket as his more general perception of avant-gardiste cultural ventures such as the Roundhouse in London or the Theatre of Ideas in New York

– venues at which somewhat unauthorised cultural manifestations appeared sporadically during the 1960s. (He doesn't mention Cedric Price's Fun Palace project of 1952, though his critique would no doubt cover this as well.) For such subversive counterculture, Pawley supposes that 'greater enthusiasm for its potential might exist' in a metropolitan situation – 'its potential' being that of anti-institutional 'happenings' and underground theatre to subvert, shock and revitalise cultural life. However, such vitality, as Pawley reminds us, is incompatible with the constraints of public or state sponsorship and must be subject, in the metropolitan case, to 'enforced closure and probable arrest'. Hence, a fortiori, the provincial version must fail. To be sure, there is little sign, as it appears today, of cultural subversion in the new town of Dronten (or reason to suppose that its Agora, at the time of its first appearance, carried any such aspiration), but it is worth noting that more than one writer[1] has wanted – perhaps a little naively – to embed COBRA and the New Babylon

Plan and section: a 'landscape' in which everyone could see and hear the same thing.

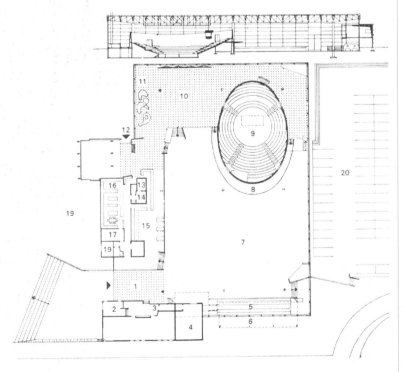

Key to ground-floor plan

1	Entrance	5	Bowling alley	9	Theatre	13	Still room	17	Larder
2	Box-office	6	Cleopatra room	10	Foyer	14	Bar service	18	Staff canteen
3	Cloakroom	7	Main hall	11	Sculpture	15	Bar	19	Terrace
4	Store	8	Ambulatory	12	Café entrance	16	Kitchen	20	Parking

Pawley's more general observation that 'Parker Morris space standards, central heating and piped water, by simply keeping people at home' have tended to promote the decline of public life amongst the lower orders may, indeed, be correct, but it is hardly, in itself, a cause for regret if such public life had been no more than a consequence of inadequate living standards. The assertive presence of those classes in what must today pass for 'public space' is demonstration, if of nothing else, of the extent to which the repressive paternalism of early postwar welfare is now a thing of the past.

A performance space with six permutations of use.

'Street' functions underscore the notion of a public (or social?) realm.

It would be wrong to see the building as dedicated primarily to cultural experiment.

At the time of its original construction, Dronten's Agora was intended to continue in use until, by the turn of the century, the town's population would have doubled from 10,000 to 20,000 inhabitants.

project of Constant Nieuwenhuys in the narrative of mainstream Dutch architecture during the 1960s. Architectural culture in the Netherlands was, undoubtedly, in advance of the UK in terms of the depth, the range and the sophistication of the critical scrutiny to which the values and procedures of postwar Modernism were subjected at that time – and subsequently.

The supposition that people will finally abandon all attempts at public appearance, deterred by individual and collective violence, by 'treachery, imprisonment by computer error, vandalism, phone tapping, brain washing, car crashes and perpetual lawsuits' (from all of which, incidentally, to remain 'private' is no protection), would be to suggest that the 'public life' whose demise it was fashionable, in 1969, to bemoan, had been a phenomenon contingent upon personal safety. 'Imperial Rome's Saturnalian heroes', whose fate Pawley equates with that of celebrities in the year 2000, were heroes precisely because they took risks. Certainly, it would be unusual, today, to open a newspaper that did not castigate some reported failure of safety as a dereliction of governmental or corporate duty, but it is, overwhelmingly, in the public consumption of their private lives that today's public figures are conspicuously tormented. In any case, Dronten's Agora was surely never envisaged as a stage for heroic or tragic events; more the sociable pleasures of karaoke than the loneliness of the misunderstood ground-breaker.

In light of what has been said, the four headings under which Martin Pawley refutes the right of the Dronten Agora to a place in a future after (or even before) the year 2000 must appear, from the perspective of 2004, to be more in the nature of general complaints about the world in which he found himself living than about a specific architectural response to a civic brief in a small Dutch new town. The reality of what the intervening years have witnessed has been, in all probability, more horrific than Pawley's projections from the experience of 1969, substantiating a profounder cynicism than his. Nevertheless, the project of the multifunctional public facility was not

abandoned in Holland during the 1970s (nor has it been since), and larger, more ambitious schemes such as Onno Greiner's centre De Flint at Amersfoort (1975–9) and the Vredenburg music centre (1979) by Herman Hertzberger have further explored Van Klingeren's notion of the type as enclosed urban space. From such examples, the UK might indeed have much to learn.

At the time of its original construction, Dronten's Agora was intended to continue in use until, by the turn of the century, the town's population would have doubled from 10,000 to 20,000 inhabitants. In the event, the interior was extensively modified in 1987, when acoustic separation between areas of different uses was installed (while, as far as possible, retaining visual continuity). When visited, in February 2003, on an architectural students' field trip, it was disappointing to find oneself too late to enjoy the architecture of its original interior, the building being half stripped in preparation for a process of upgrading and enlargement evidently in fulfilment of planning predictions made 33 years earlier. In this respect, the De Meerpaal centre has come off better, it must be admitted, than Van Klingeren's subsequent essay in the type – the mixed-use centre at 't Karregat, Eindhoven (1970–3), in which he attempted a 'universal' structural system, supposedly adaptable for any function but, in the event, now destitute of any and boarded up.

As it was originally designed and built, the De Meerpaal centre was conceived as an urban landscape, the components of which were largely defined in changes of level or surface, laid out around and beneath a 'Miesian' floating roof held on nine steel columns. Only 'servant' spaces were enclosed by walls, expressed as lower structures emerging as necessary from the glazed membrane that separated internal from external urban space. Clearly referential to Walter Gropius's Total Theatre project of 1927, the elliptical performance

The Agora in February, 2003. Parts of the original building will survive in the new, expanded centre. The performance element can be seen with its added acoustic enclosure of 1987.

element could be adapted for six types of presentation. The idealism implicit in this arrangement evidently took insufficient note of the mutual conflicts that could result from the intrusion of volley-ball players' grunting and stamping in the hushed suspense of an intimate drama, of brass-band rehearsals or the clatter of falling skittles in a dance class or a committee meeting. Hence the alterations of 1987. But Van Klingeren's chosen epithet 'Agora', evoking the representational civic space of ancient Greece – the place where, in the words of Hannah Arendt (whose thinking seems to inform the project, whether consciously or not) 'everyone can see and hear the same thing', leaves little room for doubt as to the intended role of the centre within a nascent community on newly reclaimed land where, even today, Dronten feels all of its 100 kilometres from Amsterdam. Van Klingeren's Agora was to be the focus for the construction of a local identity through participation in sporting, recreational or creative activities, the 'social condenser' of a very specifically Dutch self-awareness from which alienation, subversion or confrontation was (and, despite some alarming counter-indications, generally remains) conspicuously, enviably and, to us, quite puzzlingly absent.

Now that it exists only in the memory of architectural drawings and largely interior photographs, it seems worth noting, for the record, that Van Klingeren did a good job with the architecture of the Dronten Agora; there is a relaxed and inviting suggestiveness in the ordering of its 'landscape' that is convincingly juxtaposed with the forceful directness of the covering structure and enclosure. The architecture speaks of modernity without technological hysteria, and of civic decorum without empty rhetoric. What Martin Pawley wrote in 1969 belongs definitely to its time, articulating anxieties that were felt by many thoughtful people (as Uncle Sam the liberator came increasingly to stand for the corruption of values under a deceit of freedom). The building comes well out of comparison with a great deal of what has subsequently passed as public architecture. As for what has subsequently passed for architectural criticism – knee-jerk disapproval of all that is not either nostalgic, ironic or self-abnegating to the point of extinction, of any formal language expressive of hope for mankind or its future – one would have to say that the Agora at Dronten has had a lucky escape. ⌀

Note
1 For example, Hans Ibelings, *20th Century Architecture in the Netherlands*, Netherlands Architecture Institute (NAi), (Rotterdam), 1996 and Hans van Dijk, *Twentieth-Century Architecture in the Netherlands*, Uitgeverij 010 Publishers (Rotterdam), 1999.

Martin Pawley writes: 'Thanks for the copy of James Madge's article. I read every page with fascination! ... I cannot resist suggesting a couple more of my old ⌀ pieces that he might like to get his teeth into. There is 'Caroline Come to Canvas City Your Friend Linda Has Been Busted', my report on the 1969 Isle of Wight music festival, and also 'Architecture Versus the Movies', my special issue on EXPO'70 in Osaka, which I think appeared in June 1970. He might well see if he can track down a copy of my book *The Private Future: Causes and Consequences of Community Collapse in the West*, published by Thames & Hudson in 1973 and Pan Books in 1974.'
Samantha Hardingham writes: Well, James, even if you don't, I feel well and truly patronised on your behalf, so might suggest to readers they take up the Pawley challenge themselves.

COMPUTING WITHOUT COMPUTERS

John Frazer trained as an architect in London and at Cambridge during the 1960s and 1970s. He identified at the very earliest stages of their development how the processing power of computers might assist the design process, and then tried to imagine the effects of this on the role of the architect, the client/user and the environment. For 30 years he has confronted this issue with tireless enthusiasm through teaching, researching and designing. Here, he presents a very personal rough guide to where he has been, with a thought for where he thinks we are at now.

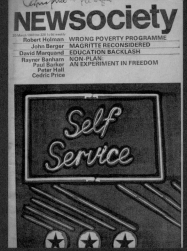

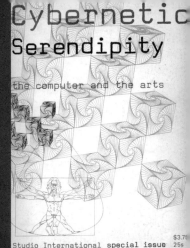

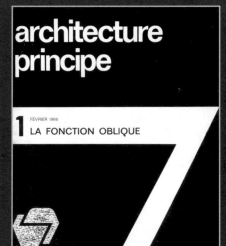

Setting the agenda – the late 1960s

Covers of the *International Dialogue of Experimental Architecture* exhibition catalogue; *Amazing Archigram 4*; the *New Society* NON-PLAN issue; the Cybernetic Serendipity exhibition, curated by Jasia Reichardt; *Auto-Destructive Art* – Gustav Metzger; *Clip Kit*, edited by Peter Murray and Geoff Smyth; and manifesto of *Architecture Principe* – Claude Parent and Paul Virilio.

The visions of the 1960s and 1970s took a long time to be realised because access to computer graphics equipment only began to become available in the late 1970s. The caption to David Green's Logplug and Rokplug (as featured in *Δ* May 1969) indicated a cable line delivering AC and DC current, telephone, international information hook-up.

By 2004, when David Greene reconstructed Rokplug as part of the Archigram exhibition in the Baltic Centre for Contemporary Art, his proposal had become technically feasible, as demonstrated by John Frazer using a wireless connected battery-powered computer to write this article, and send it to guest-editor Samantha Hardingham from his garden hammock in Sussex.

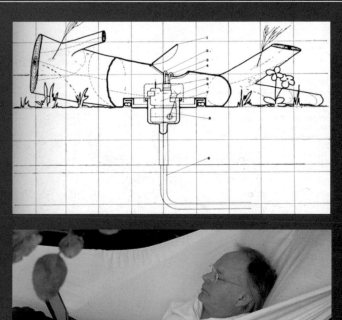

2004

I am typing this from a hammock in my garden in Sussex using a wireless-connected, battery-powered computer only dreamed of in the 1970s. The technology has at last arrived but with a staggering performance far beyond the wildest dreams of even the most optimistic gurus, and at an even more astonishingly low cost. Whilst I type this sentence, a student has logged in from China for a tutorial in one window, my son is chatting in another, and in a third window an urgent email query from Frank Gehry's office is being answered; it is 4pm British Summer Time – that magic time of the day when Los Angeles is waking up and Shanghai is not yet asleep. Here I am lying in my hammock wondering why it took so long to get connected and what we have all been doing in the meantime …

I pause for a moment to reflect on having just been connected to the People's Republic of China and the United States of America all from a hammock in the European Union with an international network of agreed protocols – the politics of this seem more wondrous than the technology. The March 1974 copy of _D_ is red with a full-cover portrait of Chairman Mao holding a red copy of _D_ in the form and classic gesture of the little red book – how did _D_ know?

Whilst some commentators made prescient technical projections (Fuller) and others social and political predictions (_New Society_), only in _D_ did the two come together and, therefore, the insight into how the advancing technology might be integrated with the changing society.

The 1968 Paris student riots saw the chance of a quick change in social injustice fail, and then fade away by 1970. By the oil crisis of 1973 a new strategy was emerging to effect social and political change, and the solution was, at least in part, in the new technology and the emerging science of cybernetics in particular. I would pick 20 July 1969 as the pivotal date, when the first step on the moon became the cliché of technological achievement and the views of the spaceship earth became a symbol for all that Buckminster Fuller had been preaching for decades.

The late 1960s and early 1970s became a prolonged thought experiment for myself and fellow students at the time. There were no affordable computers to speak of, so the only option was to imagine that they existed and imagine all the rest of the technology and social and political change necessary to realise dreams. This is what I mean by computing without computers; a mental rehearsal of what architecture and a built environment would be like at the beginning of the 21st century.

Rescuing the 1970s from the Attic

As I write this caption, I am thinking specifically of issues of _D_ that I had read and contributed to as a student and young architect. Then I realise that it is architecture that has been in the attic since the early 1970s. Key ideas on the environment, ecology, sustainability and technology transfer were shelved and archived for future use – why did this happen? When (if ever) might that future use take place? Amongst the boxes in the attic labelled 'Interbuild', 'oz', 'New Society', 'Archigram', 'Clip Kit', 'Arena' and 'AAQ', I finally find 'AD 960 –79', and restore the volumes to my bookshelves. The dust and the weight, and the solemnity of the library bindings, do not distract from the still fresh images and the lightness within the covers. A random dip into 1971 produced an inflatable tube, 250 metres long and floating on the Machsee in Hanover; an open letter from Peter Cook to Warren Chalk; an Auto-mat deployable pneumatic mat by Mark Fisher; emergency housing in Peru; a long issue on the social problems of the redevelopment of Covent Garden; and an issue on the Beaux Arts Since 1968 that reviewed the aftermath of the Paris student revolution. The magazines quickly reveal that the agenda for the

1970s had been set entirely in the 1960s. So, in order to revive the flavour of the period and according to fickle memory and some note taking at the time, the following sequence of formative events is set out – a personal 'Rough Guide to Thought Experiments'.

1963

Buckminster Fuller lectures in the Architectural Association (AA) first-year studio – he is being filmed for BBC television. He is seated on a trestle table, and stops mid-sentence every time the camera stops, only to resume again mid-sentence when the filming starts again.

1964

The Fun Palace by Cedric Price and Joan Littlewood, arguably the seminal building of the century, in development since 1958, is revealed to the public in an article by Reyner Banham. (Reyner Banham, 'People's Palaces', *New Statesman*, 7 August 1964, pp 191–2)

1965

Autodestructive Art. During his lecture at the AA, Gustav Metzger contrives for his slides to burn in the projector (the flames go down the screen giving an impression of hell). A demonstration ensues in Ching's Yard. The choreographed destruction of fluorescent tubes inspires an orgy of destruction with models, drawings, drawing boards and furniture being hurled from the studio windows overlooking the yard. I am inspired to hurl myself from the rooftop onto this participatory event (others have since admitted this feeling too), not from depression but from a sense of elation.

1966

International Dialogue of Experimental Architecture (IDEA), Folkstone. Thousands of backpacking, beach-sleeping students converge from around the world on a small hall designed for an audience of a few hundred. They hear Cedric Price talk on the Potteries Thinkbelt, Hans Hollein on the Retti candle shop and the invention of Tote bags, which takes the tiny shop out into the city, as well as Joseph Weber, Ionel Schein, Yona Freidman, Arthur Quarmby and the Archigram Group. Claude Parent and Paul Virilio speak in French in black suits, and are translated by Colin Fournier, who also rescued them from being booed off stage as they are seen as neofascist by a high-spirited audience. Reyner Banham talks on the 'End of Architecture'. Cedric Price unguardedly said that architects are

in the enclosure business, and Banham teasingly mocks this idea by using it as the launch pad for his own prophetic vision.

1967

World Design Science Decade Conference, London. Buckminster Fuller is trying to involve architectural students in this project and in his World Game on the basis that design education develops a comprehensive approach to problems whilst all other disciplines are becoming increasingly specialist. He speaks for four hours in one seamless sentence unbroken by the usual need to breathe. His generosity of spirit shows when afterwards, although visibly tired, he talks with me personally for a further hour. I have talked with Fuller four times in my life; every time was magic, every time I felt a renewed sense of purpose – yet I can't remember a single word he said.

1968

Cybernetics Serendipity, an exhibition at the ICA organised by the incredible Jasia Reichardt. A dog-eared catalogue (a special issue of *Studio International*) reveals an incredible mix: Norbert Wiener, Stafford Beer, Karlheinz Stockhausen, John Cage, Edward Ihnatowicz, Gustav Metzger, Gordon Pask – poetry, music, art, sculpture, dance, film, architecture. Page after page documents seminal experiments that set the agenda for the coming 40 years.
(Jasia Reichardt, 'Cybernetic Serendipity', Cosmorama, ⌂ September 1968, p 395)

The 1960s dream wholeheartedly embraced the idea of the general availability of computers. But the reality was that in the mid-1960s there were no graphics display devices generally available. John Frazer, as a student in 1968, plotted his final-year project on cartridge paper on a hired pen plotter with no screen graphics available.

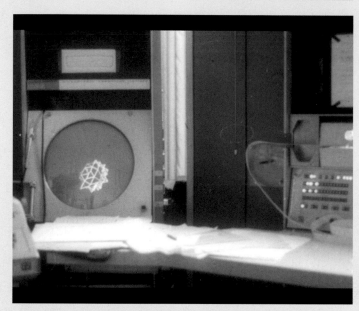

In 1969, the only screen graphics display service at Cambridge University was a circular cathode ray tube where the first lines fade before the last lines are drawn. John Frazer is now able for the first time to interact directly with a growing seed of a design that automatically reconfigures itself to spatial requirements.

Also in 1968

I do my first computer drawings plotted by pen on cartridge paper (no screen preview). Generating drawings of a geometrical complexity that is virtually impossible by hand is inspirational, but the pain of writing the software (no AutoCad yet) and entering all that data, start me on a lifelong project to improve the situation. I plot my final-year project, win the year prize for it, and all the original drawings are stolen from the end-of-year exhibition.
(John Frazer, 'Reptiles', Δ April 1974, pp 231–9)

1969

The pyrotechnics to mark the end of the 1960s take place in March when *New Society* publishes 'NON-PLAN: An Experiment in Freedom' by Reyner Banham, Paul Barker, Peter Hall and Cedric Price, setting forth a manifesto for the end of planning as we understand it. (Reyner Banham, Paul Barker, Peter Hall and Cedric Price, 'NON-PLAN: An Experiment in Freedom', *New Society*, 20 March 1969, pp 435–43)

1970

A new mood of seriousness and an urge to get the job done. This means an end to my student years and a new life as a don at Cambridge. I start to run the first year in the Architecture School with Britt Andressen (Australian Architects gold medallist) and Barry Gasson (now Sir Barry). The personal change in mood and imperative mirrors a change in society as it moves into the new decade. It is as if for a glorious 10 years the whole world has shared a formative student experience – but now we are expected to repay our debt.

Inventors, Masters, Starters of Crazes, and Diluters – so Ezra Pound classifies creative activity (Ezra Pound, *ABC of Reading*, Yale 1934, Faber 1961). The Inventors and the Starters of Crazes as I have described, resided in the 1960s. The Masters step into the foreground in the early 1970s. They use processes as well as, or better than, those who invented them, and are often combining ideas. The Diluters descend in the mid-1970s. If the 1960s is characterised by inventive spirit, the 1970s will be an era of developing mastery. The change is marked by an

Gordon Pask lecturing at the AA in 1977.

extraordinary issue of $\triangle$ guest-edited by Roy Landau and focusing on cybernetics and responsive systems with a galaxy of star contributors, including Karl Popper, Warren Brodey, Nicholas Negroponte, Stanford Anderson, David Greene, Cedric Price and Gordon Pask. This issue defines the agenda for the coming 30 years.(Royston Landau (ed), 'Thinking About Architecture and Planning', $\triangle$ September 1969, pp 478–514)

Meanwhile, I have teamed up with Alex Pike, who I know only as a regular contributor to $\triangle$, also new to Cambridge. We form a research group (including the young Ken Yeang) to investigate an ecologically responsible architecture. It is not just an academic research group; we also plan to construct a prototype autonomous house.

Also in 1970

I have gained access to a graphics display device (a circular cathode ray tube where the first lines fades before the last ones are drawn), the only one at Cambridge University. With the help of expertise in the mathematical laboratory, I start to develop generative programs based on a kind of digital DNA that enable me to generate structural forms automatically without the tedium of entering all that data.

1973

As the world economy stagnates following the oil crisis, I wander from Cambridge back to the AA, teaching again with Britt Andressen. We introduce the students to another thought experiment, asking them to construct a computer from matchboxes and coloured beads. I am subsequently afforded the pleasure of teaching for a further year with David Greene and Will Alsop.

1976

The intelligent building is born in Cedric Price's Generator project. My wife Julia and I are consultants (we are building a computer system and writing the software) on the project in order to facilitate Cedric's belief that an instantaneous architectural response to a particular problem is too slow, and that 'architecture should create desirable conditions and opportunities hitherto thought impossible'. The Generator's services and structures respond to the users' wishes with help from both a crane and computers embedded in every structural element.

1977

I take up a post as head of the School of Art and Design Research, History and Criticism in the College of Art and

Our company, Autographics, is founded, followed by software package Autoplan, launching a 20-year task to write useful software that we believe assists design rather than obstructs it. A few years later AutoCad appears, eclipsing our pioneering little company.

Design in Belfast and at last have access to the resources to introduce computing into the curriculum as the first microprocessor-based graphics system becomes available. Christmas is spent sitting in bed, snowbound, in a remote farmhouse in Killyleagh, County Down, reading a stack of manuals for the Tektronix 4051, which has just been delivered. Excitement grows as the realisation dawns that here is the potential for every architect to have a graphics computer on his or her desk, and indeed the decade is to end with the arrival of the Personal Electronic Transactor, affectionately known from their acronym as PETs. Apple and, eventually, IBM follow.

1979

Our company, Autographics, is founded, followed by software package Autoplan, launching a 20-year task to write useful software that we believe assists design rather than obstructs it. A few years later AutoCad appears, eclipsing our pioneering little company.

What Went Wrong?

Contributing factors:

1 The period suffered from the effect of two contrary tides – energy and information flowing in opposite directions (and contrary to the laws of physics). On the one hand, developments were made in technology and a profusion of ideas for ways to save the planet. On the other, the exploitation and trivialisation by three decades of visionless politics culminated in 1979 in the beginning of the Thatcher era that led to the draining of a nation's creative spirit and imagination.

2 The technology moved fast – in many ways faster than expected. The social and political and economic systems did not. When the problem becomes disconnected from the solution, we do not have a solution at all but a new problem.

3 The optimism of the period is typified by a piece by Fred Scott, 'How It's Made', lamenting the architects' reluctance to interest themselves in how things are made. He discusses CNC, the computer numerical control of machines to produce a flexible production line, quoting an article in *Science Journal*. Scott was quick to see the implications for the building industry. (Fred Scott, 'How It's Made', Cosmorama, *ᗄ* November 1968, p 507.) The line of argument was expanded by Chris Abel in 'Ditching the Dinosaur Sanctuary' (*ᗄ* August 1969, pp 419–24). However, neither Scott nor Abel engaged with the problem of the fantastic cost of these machines in relation to the time it would take to machine the parts. The vision was right, and the cost is now resolved, but the one-dimensional, uncritical awe of the technology remains unresolved.

4 The Diluters. RIBA got in early on the exploitation and dilution act with its annual conference in 1972. Under the banner of 'Designing for Survival', it pretended to be making a professional effort to address the growing energy crisis. My initial delight that RIBA was taking the environmental and energy issues seriously, and my youthful pride at being invited to speak, soon gave way to the horrific realisation that, far from taking the issue seriously, the profession just saw it as yet another exploitable opportunity. Serious issues were appropriated and trivialised to justify the irrelevancies of the formalists and the monumentalisers. I vowed never to join this demeaning self-interest group. The outcome of the conference was the RIBA 'Long Life Loose Fit Low Energy' programme. Andrew Rabeneck, Francis Duffy and John Worthington wrote an open letter to the RIBA President,

The Generator project became the world's first intelligent building. Working model of part of the interactive Generator environment with a microprocessor embedded in every element for computing its own reconfiguration. Concept, electronics, mode and software by John and Julia Frazer as cybernetic consultants to Cederic Price, 1978.

By the late 1970s, the first microprocessor-based graphics storage devices became commercially available. (Left) A Tekronix 4051 introduced by John and Julia Frazer into the Belfast College of Art & Design in 1977. By the end of the 1970s the first personal computers became available, but the screen graphics were of such low resolution that a multicolour pen plotter still had to be used for graphics output. (Right) Belfast College of Art & Design, 1977: a Commodore PET (personal electronic transactor) with 10-pen colour plotter and software designed and written by John and Julia Frazer.

The technology moved fast – in many ways faster than expected. The social and political and economic systems did not. When the problem becomes disconnected from the solution, we do not have a solution at all but a new problem.

'Universal Constructor', AA diploma 11 unit students, 1990, with Gordon Pask and Julia Frazer.

The 1990s

By 1992, all the tools are available: the computers, the software – virtual reality is a reality. The problem now shifts to one that would make connections between 30 years or more of pieces: How to integrate the new technology with the human side, the interaction, the environment and the underlying purpose. John Frazer works with students at the AA from 1990 to 1995 to build experimental interactive models, generative and evolutionary systems and use genetic algorithms and neural nets with which to explore architecture as if it were a form of artificial life. Applications include creating a participatory planning model for the citizens of Groningen – 'Universal Constructor' (AA diploma11 unit students, with Gordon Pask and Julia Frazer, 1990). Cedric Price and Gordon Pask also worked with this group, helping to make the link between formative thought processes and ongoing student discoveries. The 'Universal Interactor' exhibition (AA diploma 11 unit students, 1992) invited visitors to interact with networked input and output devices. The arrival of global access to the Internet in 1994 was celebrated by diploma 11 students in their 'Interactivator' exhibition at the AA. Here, an object evolved in the heart of the exhibition in response to input from the actual visitors, virtual visitors on the Internet and the changing environmental conditions of the exhibition space. The computing without computers experiment is re-run, although this time we have the computers. The purity of the thought experiment is all the more poignant and the imperative of doing without the encumbrance of the machine all the more powerful. Working in a virtual space is further developed when John Frazer takes up the post of head of the School of Design at the Hong Kong Polytechnic University in 1998 , where students build the Global Virtual Design Studio with which to conduct shared global projects.

'Universal Interactor' exhibition, AA diploma 11 unit students, 1992. Visitors interacting with networked input and output devices include (left to right) Ken Yeang, Britt Andressen (with daughter), Marcial Echenique, Samantha Hardingham and Sophie Hicks (back to camera).

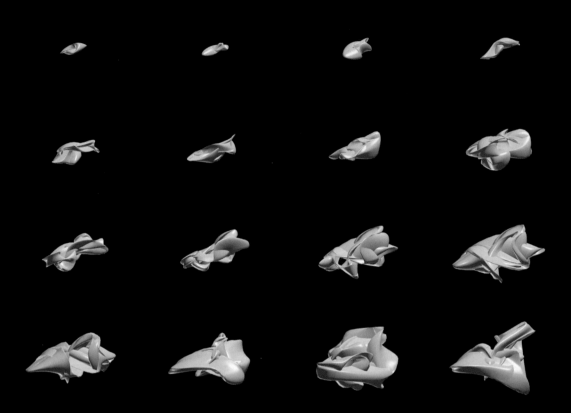

'Interactivator' exhibition, AA diploma 11 unit students, 1995. The form evolves in response to input from the actual visitors to the exhibition, the environmental conditions in the exhibition space, and input from virtual visitors on the Internet.

Global Virtual Design Studio, Hong Kong Polytechnic University, 1998.

Computers have become ubiquitous, pervasive and getting close to being invisible. So I toast the new millennium and declare myself post-digital in the sense of transcending the need to anymore talk about computers. We can take them for granted and get back to the real problems of designing a future in response to the needs of people and the environment.

Alex Gordon, expressing their 'profound sense of unease' at the way the institute was running the programme (Andrew Rabeneck, Francis Duffy, John Worthington, 'LL/LF/LE – Open letter to Alex Gordon PRIBA', Δ January 1973, p 6). The issue of participation in design was similarly obscured.

5 The dream of CAD (computer-aided design) was sold cheap as COD (computer-obstructed design) and soon collapsed into the realm of ghastly renderings that polluted every minor school of architecture's degree shows for several years.

6 The technological optimism of the late 1960s and early 1970s was one-dimensional. Many of its sources can be found in much earlier work, and the richness of the thinking seemed to get lost over time. Fuller, in writing *Nine Chains to the Moon* (1938), raised environmental issues, and published *4D Time*

Lock (1929) attacking the stagnation in the building industry. Woudhysen and Abley have only recently published *Why is Construction so Backward* (Wiley-Academy, 2004). Patrick Geddes discussed participation in his built project Citizens' Outlook Tower (1892) and Kropotkin's political influence can be found in his *Fields, Factories and Workshops* (1899).

2000

Computers have become ubiquitous, pervasive and getting close to being invisible. So I toast the new millennium and declare myself post-digital in the sense of transcending the need to anymore talk about computers. We can take them for granted and get back to the real problems of designing a future in response to the needs of people and the environment.

2005

A recent symposium on 'Architecture and Digital Integration' at the Royal Society of Arts established that the hardware and software necessary for design and computer-controlled fabrication and assembly technology has now developed to the point where the dinosaur of industrialisation by fabricating repetitive elements can finally be ditched. Software adapted out of the realms of the aerospace industry and into the domain of construction has at last displaced software written to merely speed the existing design process. The dream of software to generate, and ultimately construct, forms and spaces appropriate to a responsive and ecologically responsible future architecture, is at last with us. Examples as diverse as Gaudí and Gehry, baroque churches and gherkins, illustrated the feasibility of the technology and its necessity, or so many speakers claimed. A digital project ecosystem has been formed of a loose affiliation of architects, engineers, fabricators and builders to effect a radical reform of the construction industry including education and training.

Avid readers of Δ will have known this was coming for over 40 years. We still have the same concerns. Will the mistakes of the 1970s be repeated with a one-dimensional approach to the technology without the process and the purpose? Are we in danger of again seeing the solution out of the context of the problem? The last word to Cedric Price: 'Technology is the answer – but what was the question?'

And the Δs? – they will now be staying on my bookshelves ... Δ

PLANNING TOOLS

Evolutionary Towers, Groningen, 2003
In response to Groningen's 'High Buildings' urban policy, S333 proposed a parallel world of high buildings to coexist with the existing urban fabric. The towers 'plug into' the existing ground-level urban ecology respecting ownership boundaries, historical traces and existing physical/social conditions. To develop the proposals, S333 used advanced computer software to generate the tower models, working with Professor John Frazer, Dr Ming Xi and Professor Liu Xiyu from Shandong University, Jinan, China, establishing a series of seeding rules from which the tower models emerged.

New forms of practice that respond to the changing role of the architect are now breaking through to reveal architecture as very much a process, contrary to the profession's 30-year obsession with itself as object and surface. Much of the ground for this change was set in the 1970s. Now that the technology has arrived, **Chris Moller** talks about how the work of his own S333 epitomises the new breed of architect by addressing wider urban issues, engaging other disciplines in the design process and creating new tools with which to work.

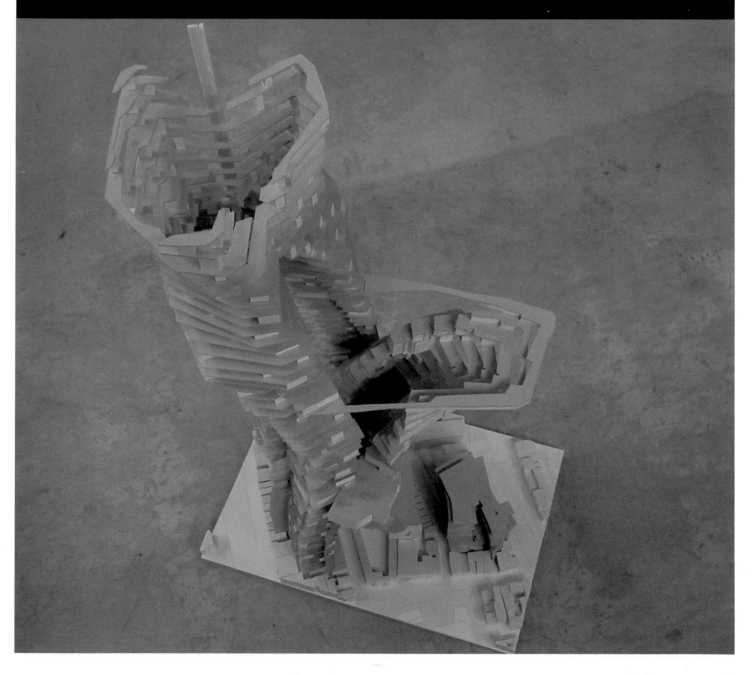

Nieuw Vennep Town Centre, Nieuw Vennep Harlemmermeer, the Netherlands, 2000–03
It is becoming increasingly clear that there is a need to begin developing tools and methods to help facilitate negotiation between different interests and stakeholders with the ambition of reaching a broader collective understanding. For the workshop series in the Nieuw Vennep project, S333 invented and built a game with rules, pieces and monetary restrictions specific to the constraints of the project. This allowed the workshop participants to begin to engage in the complexities of the plan, 'playing out' a series of potential development scenarios.

An indication of S333's interest in urbanism is literally the choice of location from which the practice has chosen to operate and function in new territories of design. The studio is based in the Netherlands, where it can benefit from the Dutch tradition of collaborative, cross-disciplinary research and realisation of projects that enables joined-up thinking across architecture, landscape, infrastructure and urban design.

Over the last decade there has been a shift by architects into urban planning and methods of organising and understanding urban processes. In Europe, urban-planning issues have been highlighted by the simultaneous emergence of the EU and its spin-offs such as Europan. The Europan organisation has successfully achieved a reputation as one of the most exciting and valuable vehicles for young architects to engage in competitions right across Europe. City municipalities and developers are eager to draw from this biannual pool of young talent to find ideas to help unlock the complexity of the urban sites chosen. Architecture is seen as a tool focused around housing as a key programmatic device to help transform areas of deprivation and dislocation.

The influence and increasing availability of computers, new technologies and the use of mobile and wireless networks, offer metaphors to architecture as identified, each in their different ways, by Marshall McLuhan, Buckminster Fuller, the Situationists, Metabolists, Archigram and Cedric Price. These thinkers attempted to understand a broader context of human existence ('the extensions of man' and 'the medium is the massage' – McLuhan). They invented new instruments and techniques and words to confront issues such as limited resources: 'How much does your building weigh?' – Fuller. Or, to pose questions on mobility: 'Should your building move?' – Archigram. Or, 'Do you even need a building?' – Price. They asked these questions to explore what the impact of buildings might be – environmental, social or psychological qualities. They helped us to shift our understanding of

architecture beyond the object, to reveal its power as verb.

We can now ask these questions once again, in the current context of changing global conditions and the necessary redefinition of the role of the architect. S333 was prompted to ask: What is your building doing? We are interested in context and urban processes and how these can be tapped or catalysed to inform both the project and its surroundings. Like Fuller or Eames, we try to apply scaleless thinking – what we call 'zooming' – to both understand potentials in the context of utilising existing materials or building processes and pushing them beyond their intended use, as well as developing compositional techniques.

In projects such as Schots 1+2 in Groningen, the Netherlands, the buildings extend and transform the ecological corridor of the adjacent park. They operate as a conduit at a number of scales and in different parts of the project by developing a landscape strategy that is not an assembly of separate figures but a woven layer through the whole complex, integrated like McLuhan's mosaic thinking: up walls, over roofs and into difficult corners. The limits of concrete tunnel construction have been challenged beyond their intended standard efficiency to address complexities in plan and section. The large structures can tune into small-scale adjacent buildings before twisting and stepping back into higher elements or absorbing the road into the bowels of the building to provide easy vehicular access to public facilities and dwellings in a project that is primarily pedestrian orientated.

The ability to see the fragility of the earth from the moon raised a global consciousness of the environment, and a global public awareness and political will has emerged. The meaning of Agenda 21, established at the Rio Conference on Global Warming, gathers momentum as some clients (especially city councils) try to change their philosophical stance.

An indication of S333's interest in urbanism is literally the choice of location from which the practice has chosen to operate and function in new territories of design. The studio is based in the Netherlands, where it can benefit from the Dutch tradition of collaborative, cross-disciplinary research and realisation of projects that enables joined-up thinking across architecture, landscape, infrastructure and urban design. The country's limited resources in terms of space, and the threat of flooding, have generated a special culture, or atmosphere, that enables separate disciplines to work collectively, and design research is thus taken seriously and supported by central government and funding agencies. Members of S333 are from a number of different countries working with an international scope of resources. Our strategy for survival is to become a new generation of pioneers, and we bring this attitude to every project. It is this pioneering spirit that drives us, even though the risks are high.

Architecture is beginning to be understood in a new way. Not in the singular sense of the quality of space itself, but rather its meaning in relation to a wider set of criteria; defining how something performs, or what it is doing in relation to a number of simultaneous urban processes. What is the role of architecture in supporting or reinforcing urban ecological issues? How does architecture perform in terms of reducing carbon production, or using and generating energy? Does architecture help to absorb or slow water run-off? These questions require an understanding of environmental challenges and a globally connected thought strategy whereby design problems are addressed simultaneously. In nature, complex multi-scaled issues are constantly resolved with surprising creativity and originality using interrelated, coevolving mechanisms and processes. Traditional design practices work in a diametrically opposing fashion where various aspects of a given project are separated as tasks for different disciplines working at different scales: traffic engineers, civil engineers, ecologists, planners etc. The architect is asked to design an object within these parameters. Such an approach does not demand that the architect be creatively engaged in designing the overarching

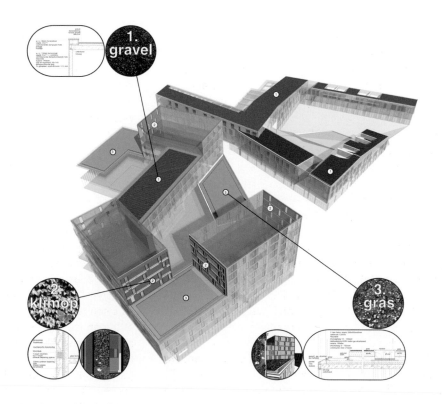

Schots 1+2, CiBoGa Terrain, Groningen, the Netherlands, 1993–2003
The grown and the made reposition themselves in Schots 1+2 as a mosaic of ingredients generating an artificial urban wilderness extending the next-door park. The multi-layering of activities and landscapes offers alternatives to the interiorised hermetic world of the traditional urban block. Inhabitants include people, insects, bats, small birds and, hopefully, butterflies. Through a continual investigation using architecture as a device to transform issues of ecology, energy, transport and polluted ground, arose a series of unexpected opportunities and an alternative way to live back in the city.

CITY
IN A ROOM

intention for the project, which is precisely the discipline in which he or she is trained.

S333 is currently working with a number of city councils to enable them to look at complex spatial and environmental problems at the scale of a whole city. For example, a research project for the city of Amsterdam reveals a different kind of quality-space for architects to operate within by unlocking the environmental limitations that restrict 66 per cent of the surface area of the city. 'Waste Space' invents a specially designed 'feedback think-model' to creatively inform an inventory of all the environmentally restricted sites across the city. Sample locations are identified. A list of ambitions for the locations is derived and combined with optimisation tools in response to specific types of environmental pollution. Thus potential design solutions are generated.

Crucial for any city is the question of how to negotiate the increasingly difficult processes required to achieve urban development with a diverse range of stakeholders, interest groups and well-informed individuals. S333 has done a number of projects that reinvent the process of engagement by thinking about appropriate ways to work with citizens and stakeholders and designing interfaces that make this activity more accessible and enjoyable, and that creatively inform the quality of the end results. In Nieuw Vennep (close to Amsterdam) the studio invented a special 3-D urban game so that we could learn from 'the Vennepers' to gain the political support necessary in order to realise their new town centre. The game unlocked the impasse between citizens and council, but also enabled all parties to discover a combination of options that they never thought possible – to achieve a quiet, green environment simultaneously with one that is urban and lively. An urban plan was ultimately approved.

Parts of the architectural profession and related disciplines are beginning to believe that in order to understand and resolve many different, and often conflicting, design issues simultaneously, they will need new instruments and methods for analysis and new tools for design. The complexity of these interrelated systems is beyond the capacity of current tools.

For example, an early prototype computer model, the 'Groningen Experiment', developed by Professor John Frazer and Chris Moller in 1996 to inform urban development in Groningen, became the point of departure for the (cityinaroom) research project developed with Pavlov Medialab, Onix Architects and Peter de Kan, that asks people instead of computers to do the real-time generational processing to evolve a virtual city. In becoming part of the processing mechanism, participants started to understand the evolution of cities in new ways.

Other research projects such as the 'Evolutionary Tower', again working with Professor Frazer, in collaboration with Dr Ming Xi and Professor Liu Xiyu, in China, are based on principles from his seminal work *An Evolutionary Architecture* (Architectural Association, 1995). The Evolutionary Tower derives from designing seeding instructions for growing a building that can change and adapt to its environment rather than designing a building as a finished object from the outset. The same set of instructions can be tested in completely different kinds of environments. To use Frazer's example: different oak tree seeds will grow up to form different-shaped trees according to the particular location and environmental conditions. The same set of seeding instructions could inform different possible 'what if?' versions of how the Evolutionary Towers could evolve. The S333 website (www.s333.org/projects) shows two different versions of the project which are informed by the same set of seeding instructions – a virtual model (computer response developed by researchers in China), and a physical model built by graduate architects within the studio.

The testing of tools of this kind, and subsequently new forms of architectural practice, are currently under way on a range of projects; from large-scale planning strategies in northern England and urban development projects in the Baltics, Norway and Singapore, to social housing in East London and new types of inner-city housing in New Zealand. ∆

City In a Room, Pavlov Medialab, Pudding Factory, Groningen, the Netherlands, November 2003
(Opposite and above) In a 24-hour multimedia jam, shifts of multidisciplinary teams were invited to think, build and seek to express John Frazer's thought experiment, 'Computing without computers', in real time. In this steaming pot we collect ingredients for an evolutionary city that are passed from shift to shift by the principle of Chinese whispers; and then stirred

to taste. This experiment doesn't aim for a utopian image; it seeks to bring together the dynamic powers that are at work in cities and reflect on the unpredictable outcome. This means a change in the attitude of the designer. It is no longer the design that steers the behaviour, but the other way around. Grow with the flow.

The Info-Urbanisation of

China

For indicators as to how high-speed development responds to massive growth in population, all eyes look to China. Tim Jachna describes how the Chinese government intends to learn from the technological teething troubles of the West, and bypass them altogether by investing heavily in a digitally networked urban culture. This means drawing a much closer link between rural and urban populations until they blend into one.

All images
Scenes from the info-urban commonplace: seminal sites of the new Chinese city.

Spaces in-between: urban–rural interpenetration in the Pear River Delta. Transport corridors bind together the regional city.

Since the early 1990s, each year an average of 20 new cites have been founded in China. This trend is expected to last until 2020, to keep up with an expected near-doubling of the Chinese urban population by that time. Parallel to this, the Chinese government has been investing intensively in Internet and digital communications development since 1994. China is already the world's largest mobile telephone market and is set to become the world's largest Internet market.

If industrialisation and deurbanisation were the rallying points of the last Chinese cultural revolution, causing the depopulation of cities and the dispersal of urbanites to the rapidly industrialising countryside, informatisation and urbanisation are the two processes in which the Chinese government is currently putting its hopes for economic development. The revolution continues, by other means but with equal fervour.

The intention is to 'leapfrog' directly from an industrial society with a sparse communications infrastructure to a digitally networked urban culture, bypassing the stages in between. Villages that may previously have possessed a single telephone line have turned into wired metropolises within a decade. Too rapid and unstudied to learn from the mistakes of the West, too different in its context to repeat these mistakes, this process of info-urbanisation is producing a physical/virtual urbanism unique to 21st-century China.

The Interactive Megalopolis

The sheer infrastructural enormity of this urbanisation programme is mitigated by an organisational schema of vast, intensely networked 'interlocking metropolitan regions' (Zhou 1991). The goal is an 'interactive megalopolis' in which telecommunications and high-speed transport networks allow a regional group of cities to function as nodes in a mutually supporting network, 'jumping over' intervening areas of high

Place-making: excavation in Guangzhou.

day-to-day interactions. By this mode of reckoning, traditional road and rail transport gives these urban regions a radius of just over 100 kilometres. Proposed high-speed magnetic train systems would extend this to almost 500 kilometres, allowing each of these cities to become the core of an 'interactive megalopolis' 1,000 kilometres across (Maglev 2001), large enough to swallow up France, Germany or the UK.

The Dragon's Head cities are also China's gateways to the global Internet. All Internet traffic into and out of China passes through servers in Hong Kong, Shanghai and Beijing; 47 per cent of all mainland (excluding Hong Kong) China's websites are based in Shanghai, Beijing and Guangzhou (China Internet Network Information Center 2004), which together account for only about 2 per cent of the country's population. Urbanisation and access to digital communications technologies are practically mutual prerequisites in modern-day China and follow isomorphic distribution patterns, adding yet another layer to the polarisation between China's cities and rural areas. If the info-urbanisation programme is to affect the whole nation and not just the already privileged metropolises, the 'urban message' will have to be received far beyond even these extensive urban zones.

The cultural and technological potential for a distance-independent 'virtual megalopolis' centred on each of the Dragon's Head cities is already given. Like a long series of construction, transportation and communications innovations before them, digital communications technologies enable the continued expansion of urban regions and urban influence, while at the same time providing potential sites in their own right, hosting venues that may be seen to duplicate, parallel or supersede places in the physical world, such as the many chatrooms, online shops, virtual campuses and offices, and collaborative workspaces already frequented by Internet users. The extension of urban influence and amenities beyond the distance threshold at which the 'info-' component of info-urbanism must take over from traditional 'urban' measures, will increase to the extent that digital communications technologies become available to the still often miserably backward further-flung reaches of China.

Chinese Planning Culture

New cities in China are currently being seeded by removing barriers to the latent economically motivated 'will to urbanisation' so strongly repressed through much of Chinese history. Beijing directs provincial governments to turn certain towns, villages or rural areas into cities, and then selectively lifts restrictions for private enterprises who want to develop property

cultural or environmental sensitivity. The proposal resembles the 'regional city' concept in which the pattern of urban development takes on the form of a polycentric urban tissue (Calthorpe et al 2001).

While in theory this urban model may seem to tend towards a homogeneous urban spread, interactive megalopolises emerging in China are centred around three so-called 'Dragon's Head' cities in the north (Beijing), centre (Shanghai) and south (contested by Guangzhou and Hong Kong) of the country's coast, bolstering, rather than dissipating, the pre-eminence of these cities (Tang 2004). The potential scale of these emerging megalopolises has been defined by a commute of around 90 minutes from the Dragon's Head at the centre to the periphery, representing the effective reach of real-time

here, and rural peasants who agree to live in these cities (Liu *et al* 2003). The quickness with which cities like Shenzhen have sprung up and grown to a size of several million inhabitants attests to the strength of the urban urge, manifested as the sum of millions of individual urges for economic gain and betterment.

Chinese government urban-planning policy has tended to be reactive rather than proactive, characterised by laissez-faire policy punctuated with strict controls to rein-in out-of-control development. Chinese urbanism is a 'wait-and-see' process in which the city unfolds as a real-time self-simulation. Before the planning reforms of 1978, urban planning in China was carried out at only two scales: the master plan and the detail plan. Since then, different cities have introduced various intermediate planning levels, but gaps remain (Tang 2000). These gaps in the temporal and scalar facets of Chinese urban-planning practice are sites where private developers and individuals operate with a minimum of government control. Even at the vernacular level, the Chinese ingenuity for exploiting the spaces in-between rigid structures of control in the city can be observed in many literal and metaphorical manifestations, from the illegal urban structures atop buildings and under flyovers, to the black market in counterfeit and pirated goods.

The Floating Population

Until 1978, the Chinese population was divided into 'agricultural' and 'non-agricultural' sectors, to facilitate control of the growth of cities and movement of people. A household registration (*hukou*) system allowed food rationing and regulation of rural–urban migration. The relaxation of *hukou* restrictions in 1978 created a new class of people in Chinese society. No longer fixed to a single location, members of this 100-million-strong 'floating population' migrate between their rural homes and their more lucrative, if menial, urban jobs. Internal migrants make up a large proportion of the population of many cities, such as an estimated 3.3 million of Beijing's 11 million inhabitants (Weiss 1995). They represent a large part of the forecasted urban population growth in China and provide most of the labour for the construction of these cities.

To date, Internet access has been restricted to the same demographic of well-off professionals as in most countries. This is a large market in China, concentrated mainly in the major urban centres, but one that leaves out the majority of the country's population, and one that some say is approaching saturation. The mobile

phone network, much more prevalent than Internet access amongst marginalised groups, seems better poised to become the virtual venue of choice for the greater part of the Chinese population. Service providers looking for a new target demographic are beginning to tailor some of their services for the floating population, and it was estimated that in 2003, 60 to 70 per cent of new mobile phone service subscribers were migrant workers (China Economy 2003).

Modes of Control

Though eager for the economic benefits to be gained from e-commerce, the Chinese government is apprehensive of the political and social consequences of opening up this virtual back door to their cities. Government control is exercised in a multitude of ways (China's Internet Regulations 2000; Mueller and Tan 1997). The profusion of small, privately run Internet cafés that sprang up in the 1990s have largely been shut down and replaced with chains run by large companies that collaborate with the government. Internet cafés are required to keep an online log of all user activity for three months, to register the name and national citizen ID number of each customer, to actively transmit information to police surveillance centres and to install software blocking access to hundreds of thousands of sites.

The digital Chinese city has its own version of traffic control, as when Internet transmission speed is reduced before politically sensitive dates or after certain events, to slow down and better monitor the flow of nonofficial information. It has its own beat cops, in the form of the 30,000 people (as of 2002) employed by the government to monitor websites, chatrooms and private emails (Hermida 2002). Just as independent newspapers are banned from the kiosks of the city, all news websites must carry the state news feed and none other. Administrators of chatrooms and bulletin boards self-censor by erasing controversial posts to avoid trouble.

Virtual Communities

However, Chinese urbanites' ingenuity for adopting the spaces in-between to their own needs, guides them in finding venues in the digital city for social interaction and communication not possible in the physical city. More and more of the social life of the city unfolds in the digital dimension. The Internet is beginning to be perceived as an alternative place, where things are possible that are not allowed in traditional urban space. Events banned from the physical city, like a planned memorial service for a student murdered just before the eleventh anniversary of the Tiananmen Square massacre, have been held in online forums (Neumann 2001). Despite the government's strict monopoly in news reporting, weblogs and chatrooms blur the boundary between private conversation and reporting, and have become the de facto news source of many.

Within the range of typologies of digital places, different nominally neutral online forums have come to be associated with different socially constructed modes of use in Chinese urban life. Chatrooms have become places to set up meetings and sexual liaisons in physical space. Because the authors of weblogs can be easily traced, these sites tend to be used for innocuous banter rather than for the airing of personal opinions. Bulletin boards are the most popular places for political discussion, because of the relative anonymity of the participants, leading some social and political groups to meet online instead of in the physical space of the city. Freeness of expression seems to be proportionate to the anonymity and mobility of the venue. Digitally mediated spaces of communication and community have a complex and mutually forming relation with practices in the physical space of the city. The full consequences of this for digital and physical urban form, in China as elsewhere, are just beginning to become evident.

The primary cyber-geographical fact of China is the so-called 'Great Firewall'. Analogous to its ancient namesake, the firewall is conceived as a barrier protecting Chinese culture against foreign incursions, categorically blocking access to sites with forbidden content, usually defined as information on sensitive topics such as democracy movements or the Tibet issue. However, ways are found to subvert even this restriction. In a concrete example of the global digital city in actual practice, proxy servers outside of China circumvent the Great Firewall and the Internet police to provide access to Chinese Internet users to some of these forbidden sites.

Just as the physical and digital places of China's cities exist in a state of interdependency, the information flow that sustains and defines social groups is dependent on a fluid interplay between digital media and human agents. Because of the many government constraints, 'human relays' are very important links in the chain of communication. It is typical in China that news about events is spread through a city first by individuals using digital technologies before being announced by the government, as was the case in Guangzhou in 2002, when the SMS message 'a fatal strange flu is spreading in our city' was forwarded 40 million times daily during the first three days of the SARS outbreak. Chinese students abroad or members of expatriate Chinese communities serve as 'human proxies', forwarding content from forbidden websites (Glaser 2003). The incomplete, uneven distribution of access to digital communications is another barrier that is being overcome by human agents taking over where digital networks run out. In a United Nations Development Programme initiative, Internet terminals are set up in rural schools, so that students become 'information multipliers', spreading information pertinent to their agricultural way of life to their families and communities (Hughes and Wacker 2003, p 50).

Icons of the info-urban revolution: computers and PDA's on display in Guangzhou.

Conclusion

Though founded on separate inherited or borrowed concepts of physical and digital networks, the processes and environments of urbanisation and informatisation are concomitant and colluded in the economic development programme currently under way in China, and in the daily lives of urban Chinese. Patterns of info-urbanisation arise from the interplay between structures of government control and social practices of inhabitation and use of physical and digital venues. Digital and physical measures meld inseparably into a single phenomenon of info-urbanisation.

Today's China is a laboratory from which a new brand of 21st-century urbanism is emerging, based on an unprecedented combination of cultural, technological, political, social and economic factors. The children of the current floating population, representing a large and growing sector, will become the first generation truly at home in the emerging info-urbanised Chinese society: the model citizens of these cities. The modes of info-urbanisation that will come to define 21st-century Chinese urban civilisation will be the modes that best address the lived reality of this demographic group. ⌂

References

Calthorpe, Peter et al, The Regional City: New Urbanism and the End of Sprawl, Island Press (Washington DC), 2001.

China Economy (China Economic Information Network), 'Unicom Sells Cheaper Prepaid cdma Cards', 3 July 2003. Retrieved from ce.cei.gov.cn.

China Internet Network Information Center, 13th Statistical Survey on the Internet Development in China, Beijing, January 2004.

China's Internet Regulations (English translation of document published by Xinhua State News Agency, 1 October 2000).

Glaser, Mark, 'China's Internet Revolution', 13 November 2003. Retrieved from www.ojr.org.

Hermida, Alfred, 'Behind China's Internet Red Firewall', 3 September 2002. Retrieved from www.bbc.co.uk.

Hughes, Christopher R. and Gudrun Wacker (eds), China and the Internet: Politics of the Digital Leap Forward, Routledge (London), 2003.

Maglev Feature Story, 'Megalopolises / Interlocking Metropolitan Regions in China', 19 March 2001. Retrieved from www.magplane.com.

Mueller, Milton and Zixiang Tan, China in the Information Age: Telecommunications and the Dilemmas of Reform, Praeger (Westport, CT), 1997.

Neumann, A Lin, 'The Great Firewall', January 2001. Retrieved from www.cpj.org.

Liu, Shenghe et al, Scenario Analysis on Urbanisation and Rural-Urban Migration in China, Institute of Geographic Sciences and Natural Resources Research, Chinese Academy of Sciences (Beijing), August 2003.

Weiss, Julian M, 'A floating population: migration and culture shock in China', The World & I, Vol 10, No 12, December 1995, pp 220–26.

Tang, Wing-Shing, 'Chinese urban planning at fifty: an assessment of the planning theory literature', Journal of Planning Literature, Vol 14, No 3, February 2000.

Tang, Wing-Shing, Interview by the author, 4 March 2004.

Zhou Yixing, 'The metropolitan interlocking region in China: a preliminary hypothesis', in N Ginsburg et al (eds) The Extended Metropolis: Settlement Transition in Asia, University of Hawaii Press (Honolulu), 1991, pp 89–111.

IT'S ALL ABOUT GETTING WHAT
WHAT WE WANT IS TO MAKE W

Today we live in a culture of institutionalised public realm – it is not the grass-roots activity of the 1970s. However, **Liza Fior**, **Katherine Clarke** and **Sophie Handler** of muf architecture explain how the collaborative nature of the practice, both internally and in its approach to any project brief, defines how, today, a community is as strong as the questions it is prepared to ask of itself.

Adrian Sampson described how Jeremy Dixon designed a space at the base of some public housing for a playgroup. When, on completion, the space remained empty, Dixon found a playgroup to occupy it. Occupation, therefore, became part of a definition of fit-for-purpose.

During the Conservative era, design of the public realm was called 'community architecture' and assumed a marginal position and status. Under the New Labour government, the practices of resistance, participation and community involvement have been embraced and have become policy and orthodoxy.

The practice of community architecture was traditionally the redirecting of the architects' resources to directly engage with the users of their projects. This shift has now been enscripted in law: much funding comes with the caveat that it must be demonstrated that the community was involved in the process of allocating it. This empowerment carries its own form of poll tax – the unpaid attendance at meetings for those living in an area.

muf begins a project by uncovering the specificities of a situation with the aim of avoiding the generic in order to give projects accuracy; for example, advice on public speaking and choosing one person to direct a presentation. The practice acknowledges that the research methods are not exhaustive and sometimes begin with casual encounters and a willingness to be led, quite literally, astray by conversations 'in the field'. This wilful intuition can reveal people's multiple connections to the landscape of a place that might otherwise remain hidden. The value of that spoken narrative is the idiosyncrasy of both content and form. What is told and the telling. The segue between what is real but not necessarily meaningful, what is meaningful but not necessarily real, as well as

YOU WANT
ORK THAT FITS

the experience of the listener, which elides between what I believe and what you believe. The recognition of a relationship with the world no less than mine, but without the thoughts I think.

Architecture as practised by the auteur has always been about getting what you want, from the manipulation of the ground plane to ensuring your client is your client, to simply trying to get it right.

PUMPKIN LOGIC
2002

Location: International Convention Centre, Birmingham
Commission: Temporary installation to present the relationship between public art and regeneration
Client: Public Arts Development Trust

Is there a relationship between art and regeneration? In this project, 200 pumpkins were positioned at the entrance to the Urban Summit 2002 in Birmingham. On two monitors, two more pumpkins engaged in dialogue. Their scripts were drawn from multiple players, from artists to the residents of areas subject to regeneration, politicians, community workers and activists. Each selected quote was turned into a question and some questions of our own inserted.

Questions from the soundtrack included the following:

When you change the fabric of a place where people live, are you changing their identity and do they perceive it as an attack on their intrinsic selves? Is the idea of an art project with a local community based on a natural truth of friendship, rather than a funding agenda, simply a fantasy?

Does art give people the opportunity to go on the kinds of adventures that we just don't get the chance to go on anymore?

Art can make its way into a community and give people a voice, but can it make them say the things other people might want to hear?

Does art create a sense of community and identity in the face of social fragmentation because art makes everything equally outside the norm?

Why are artists legitimised to undertake acts of social engineering that politicians can only dream of?

Is the choreographing of others' desires and experience the artists' process and their product?

Is there a private art for rich people who want to own the objects of art, and a public or state art for others who have the experience of culture?

Is it because art works best on the margins of society, judged only by an aesthetic standard and unburdened by expectations that it should be relevant, that it is so enthusiastically promoted by the government as a tool in social exclusion?

Artists have to proceed by negotiation otherwise they are left so far outside that they have nothing to work with; is this why they are considered such a useful tool in social exclusion?

Is the worst thing about life hoping it will be different?

When a project hasn't gone well, is it like being in a relationship with a boyfriend who hates you, and all his family hate you, and all his friends hate you, and you hate them but you're just too scared to leave?

Can art negotiate problems and act on contingency in a way that in other professions would be seen as failure?

Is art obedient to an integrity you often can't understand when you're actually doing it?

Will murals always be with us?

TILBURY PARK & HORSES TAIL, COMPLETION 2004

Broadway Estate, Tilbury, Essex
Commission: design for a park and open-ended research into land use and ownership
Client: Thurrock Borough Council

These were two parallel projects: one a commission to design a small park within a housing estate, the other a piece of open-ended research entitled 'The Horses Tail'. On the first visit to the site we noticed horse dung in the children's playground – the informal and semi-legal use of the site had not been mentioned in the brief. We began by organising a gymkhana – formalising, legitimising and amplifying the presence of horses for an afternoon. This move was concretised in the final scheme, in which planted trapions (reinforced turfed rubble walls) secure the park from the cars that previously were regularly crashed into the centre of the site, but also delineate different areas for under-5s, a playground fragmented into a series of pockets to prevent dominance by a single group, and a dressage arena for the horses kept by some residents on adjoining land.

   muf began 'The Horses Tail; project within the confines of a historical investigation: looking to document, with local schoolchildren, the presence of these wandering ponies through stories gathered and mapped into layers on a digital archive. But the project gets drawn aside and the production of an archive, like the project itself, has turned into something else altogether. A group of primary schoolchildren start fabricating horse heads and bodies out of card and fleece – costumes for acting out these stories in their literal setting. A horse (with two children inside) walks across Tilbury. It is photographed performing along its route, and the photographs are made into posters that are displayed across Tilbury, beginning to question people's relationship to their surrounding landscape. 'Does a horse need a field?' 'Does a field need a horse?'

   The ponies represent a desire for a relationship to the land that exists outside the conventional organisation of social order, laying emotional claims that test regulated, prescribed definitions of land use. Can you belong to a place that you only ever move through? Can you lay claim to a place that isn't even yours?

   In August 2004, a group of schoolchildren dressed in a horse costume follow the line of a real horse as it makes its way through Tilbury from marshland, through the town, and the estate, to inaugurate the dressage arena in the new park, making room, literally, for the presence within a landscape of what is otherwise strategically suppressed.

'OPEN SPACES THAT ARE NOT PARKS WITH AN EMPHASIS ON YOUTH' 2004

Location: Newham, Greater London
Commission: to work with local residents, including young people, to identify small open spaces suitable for investment, devising programmes for these spaces, and identifying sources of funding
Client: London Borough of Newham

How do you make space for the diverse desires and needs of young people? There is a gendered bias implicit in standardised youth provision that is based on 'activity': the provision of sports facilities, for instance, that is more about young men than it is about young women (the underlying premise here being to re-channel the violent, antisocial energy of boys specifically). Girls we spoke to made more modest claims, wanting simply a place to sit and talk – a less active, less visible desire.

   We came across these young women sitting on the steps of a pedestrian bridge – an ideal place to meet, they told us, simply because it is 'sheltered from the wind', 'very social' and 'it's impossible to be watched by your parents ... sitting here you can honestly say you are on your way home'. Other sites identified included underpasses (again, sheltered spaces) and an alleyway frequented by girls only (opposite a male-dominated snooker hall). They told us that though they would like to, they could not (being too intimidated) enter this snooker club, where most of their male peers go. Instead, they end up congregating in nearby alleyways, troubling the perception of girls out on the streets. These streets, imagined as ideal (public space), are unlike the street ideal that feels altogether more complex. 'You say public space', say the girls, 'but if girls are seen sitting on a wall they'll automatically think you're a ho. 'The architect finds a role in turning this street-based expertise into a brief, a challenge and a proposal. △D

The following pieces form part of a series of works that Nic Clear refers to as
'scatological drawings'. These use the basic format of a CAD layout to develop
narrative themes, albeit within an abstract compositional framework. Specifically
developed to accompany the text, the three drawings shown here are constructed
through the juxtaposition of various cultural references taken from the text, from

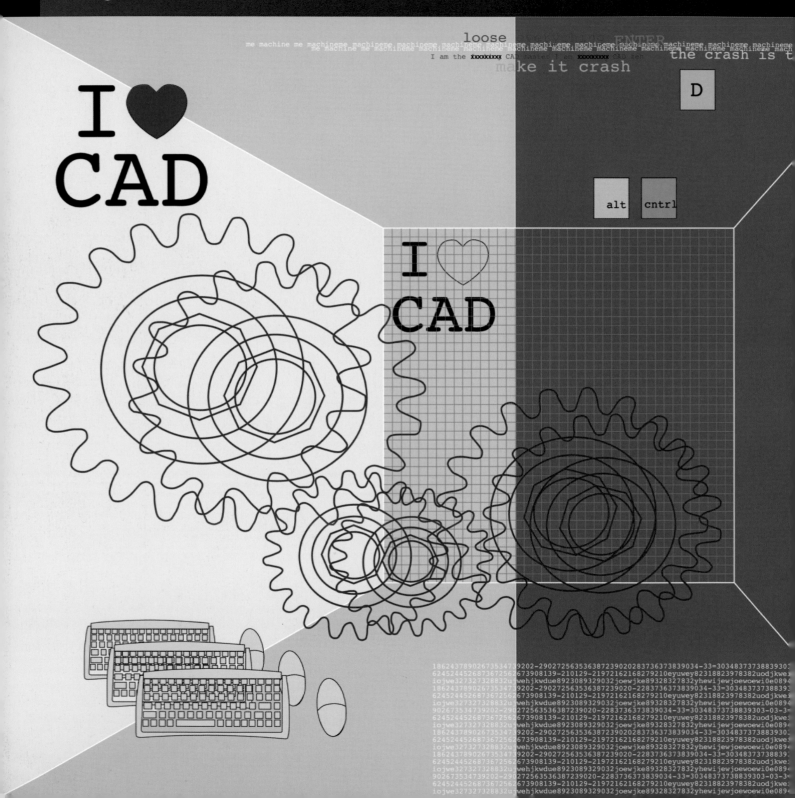

pornography to ironmongery details, graphically constructed by adapting formal organising principles based on perspectival and orthographic projections and parodying GUI layouts. The effect is to create something Clear calls 'General Dis-Arrangement drawings'.

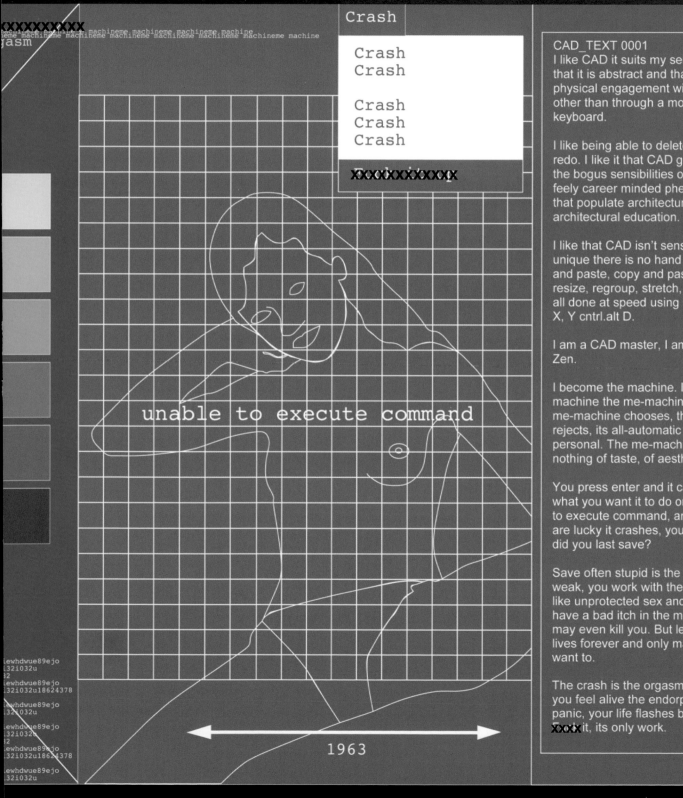

XXXXXXXXXX
neme.machine machineme.machineme.machineme.machineme.machine
neme machineme machineme machineme machineme machineme machine
gasm

Crash

Crash
Crash

Crash
Crash
Crash

XXXXXXXXXXXX

unable to execute command

1963

iewhdwue89ejo
i32i032u
32
iewhdwue89ejo
i32i032u18624378
iewhdwue89ejo
i32i032u
iewhdwue89ejo
i32i032u
iewhdwue89ejo
i32i032u
32
iewhdwue89ejo
i32i032u18624378
iewhdwue89ejo
i32i032u

CAD_TEXT 0001
I like CAD it suits my sensibilities. I like that it is abstract and that there is no physical engagement with the work other than through a mouse and a keyboard.

I like being able to delete, undo and redo. I like it that CAD goes against all the bogus sensibilities of the touchy feely career minded phenomenologists that populate architecture, especially in architectural education.

I like that CAD isn't sensitive, it isn't unique there is no hand at work. Copy and paste, copy and paste, group resize, regroup, stretch, change colour all done at speed using shortcuts, C, V, X, Y cntrl.alt D.

I am a CAD master, I am xxxxx CAD Zen.

I become the machine. I am the machine the me-machine. The me-machine chooses, the me-machine rejects, its all-automatic nothing personal. The me-machine thinks nothing of taste, of aesthetics.

You press enter and it can either do what you want it to do or it cant, unable to execute command, and then, if you are lucky it crashes, you crash. So when did you last save?

Save often stupid is the motto of the weak, you work with the auto save off its like unprotected sex and yes you will have a bad itch in the morning and it may even kill you. But lets face it no-one lives forever and only maniac would want to.

The crash is the orgasm it's only then you feel alive the endorphin rush, the panic, your life flashes before your eyes. xxxx it, its only work.

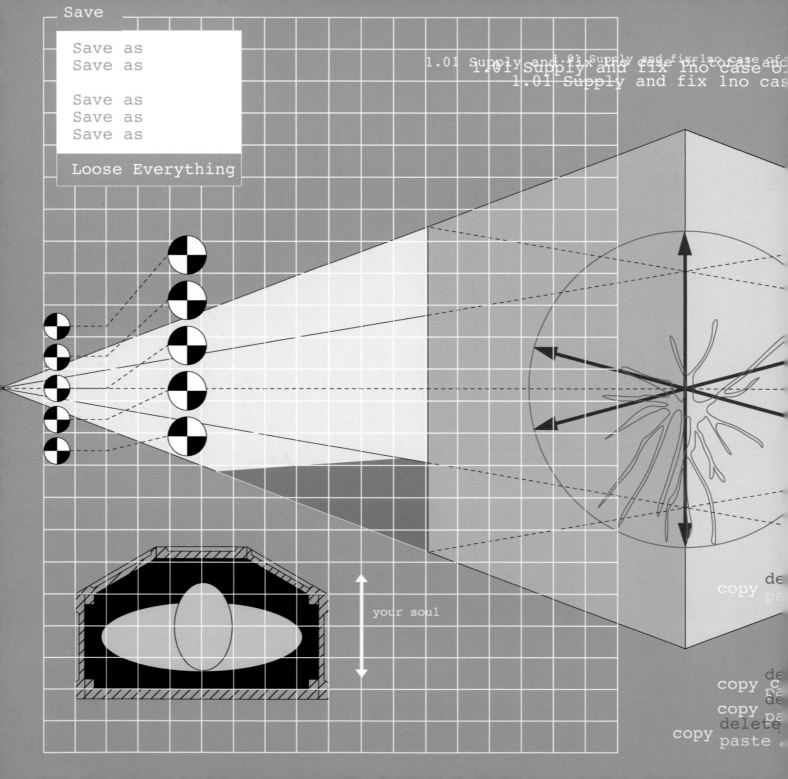

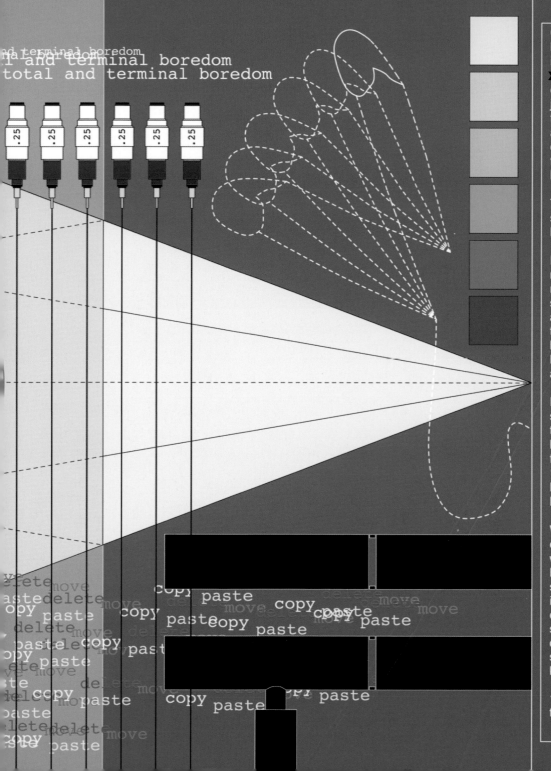

total and terminal boredom

CAD_TEXT 0002

Make it crash, put in too much information, make it do stupid things and XXX around with every parameter, loose everything. Losing work doesn't matter just do it again its always easier second time around, even if the file is corrupted and you wonder did you make a back-up did you save as. Who cares its not the finished product that matters its becoming the me-machine.

The more work you have put into something the greater the thrill of loosing it.

I used to draw by hand, I used to keep my pens really clean it was like a religious ceremony; it was like making sure I always had clean underwear and a clean cock. I was defined by the fact that my .25 Rotring never left messy blobs on the paper, that my lines and my lettering were neat and crisp I wasn't anal I was just an XXXXXX.

I drew for money an hourly rate so many sheets a day. My details were well thought out and practical. I didn't even know I was designing my own coffin from the inside with chamfered edges, a 12mm shadow gap and stainless steel D-Line handles it was really tasteful and looked good in the magazines.

When I first went mechanical I still clung onto the idea of designing the coffin. I was organised and precise, I set up libraries of details and of symbols I saved as, I renamed every drawing issue, everything was carefully organised on my hard drive and on the server. I didn't realise I had moved from designing my coffin to actually specifying the disease that was going to kill me.

1.01 Supply and fix 1 number case of total and terminal boredom

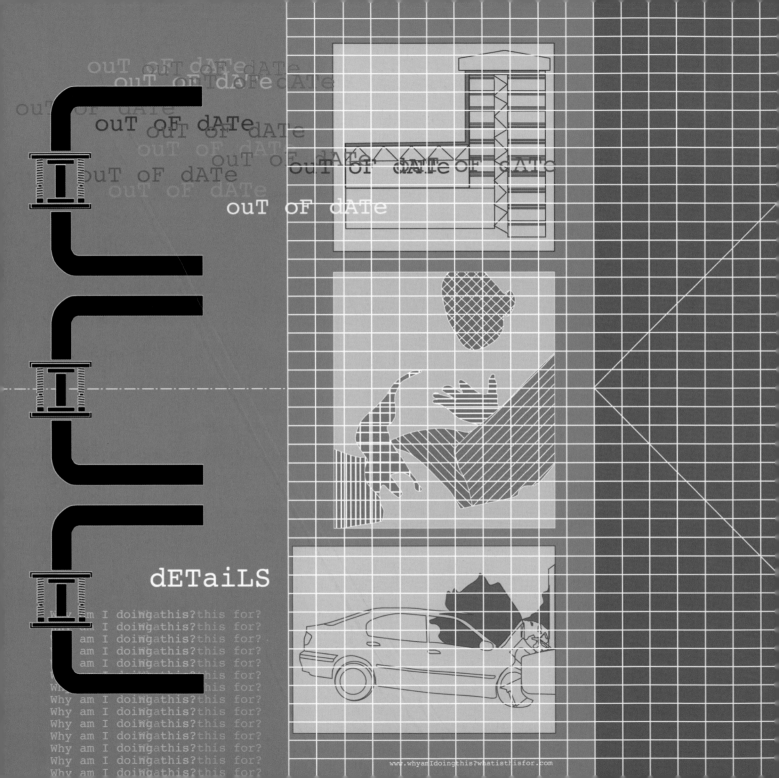

ouT oFTedAТedATe
ouT oFTedAТedATe
ouT oF dAТe
ouT oF dAТe
ouT oF dAТe dАТe
ouT oF dAТe dАТe
ouT oF dAТe
ouT oF dАТe oF dАТe
ouT oF dАТe

ouT oF dАТe

dETaiLS

Why am I doingathis?this for?
am I doingathis?this for?
am I doingathis?this for?.
am I doingathis?this for?
am I doingathis?this for?
am I doingathis?this for?
Why am I doingathis?this for?
Why am I doingathis?this for?
Why am I doingathis?this for?
Why am I doingathis?this for?
Why am I doingathis?this for?
Why am I doingathis?this for?

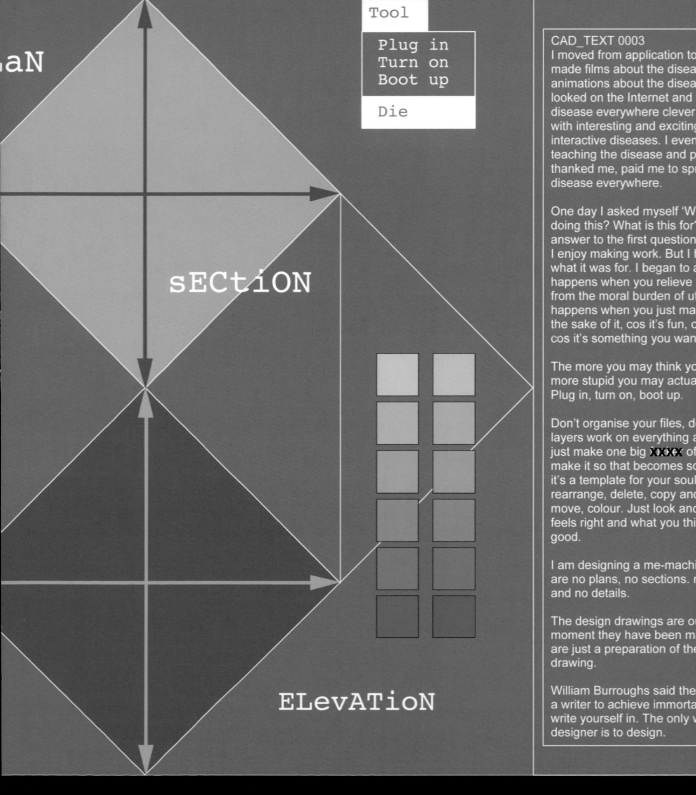

aN

sECtiON

ELevATioN

CAD_TEXT 0003
I moved from application to application I made films about the disease, I made animations about the disease, and I looked on the Internet and found the disease everywhere clever web sites with interesting and exciting uses of interactive diseases. I even began teaching the disease and people thanked me, paid me to spread the disease everywhere.

One day I asked myself 'Why am I doing this? What is this for?' The answer to the first question was simple I enjoy making work. But I had no idea what it was for. I began to ask what happens when you relieve yourself from the moral burden of utility? What happens when you just make work for the sake of it, cos it's fun, cos it's cool, cos it's something you want to do?

The more you may think you know the more stupid you may actually become. Plug in, turn on, boot up.

Don't organise your files, don't use layers work on everything at one time just make one big **xxxx** of a drawing, make it so that becomes so confusing it's a template for your soul. Then rearrange, delete, copy and paste, move, colour. Just look and do what feels right and what you think looks good.

I am designing a me-machine and there are no plans, no sections. no elevations and no details.

The design drawings are out of date the moment they have been made. They are just a preparation of the next drawing.

William Burroughs said the only way for a writer to achieve immortality is to write yourself in. The only way for a designer is to design.

On Surrealism and Architecture

{ With Some Stylistic Apologies } to André Breton

In one of the rare pieces in this issue to address the turn, or, rather, clash of architectural events of the latter part of the decade, Jon Goodbun and David Cunningham mark the occasion with a tribute to the 1978 issue of △ entitled 'Architecture & Surrealism', which highlights that whatever the dominant dogma at the time, thankfully there is always more than one way to view a collage and cacophony of thought and material.
First, though, take a position.

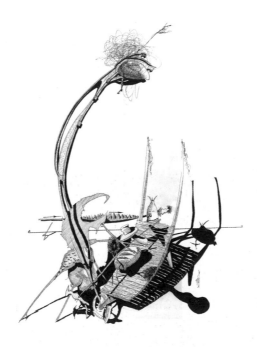

Neil Spiller plays with poetics and technology, form and myth, in utopian narrative spaces
that can be usefully considered in relation to the surrealist project.

While his house collapses and he stands amazed
before the singular packing-cases
Sought after by his bed with the corridor and the staircase
The staircase goes on without end.
— André Breton, *Le Facteur Cheval*

We, who like nothing more than youthful enthusiasms, are anxious to celebrate in this issue of *Δ* the 26th anniversary of *Δ* Profile 11, 'Surrealism and Architecture'.[1] We offer homage here to Dalibor Vesely, the mastermind of a publication that might have made such an impression on those who came after. We say 'might', for our celebration is also, of necessity, a kind of mourning of missed opportunity, of a chance meeting that never quite happened, either on the dissection table of the drawing board or in the haunted spaces of built form.

1978: the year also of 'Dada and Surrealism Reviewed' at the Hayward Gallery in London, with Colquhoun and Miller's proliferating half-cylinders providing the material support for Edward Wright's 'collages' of 'original material'. (We will forever regret that we were too young to see them). If the Hayward curators gathered together remnants of *La Révolution Surréaliste*, *Documents* and *Minotaure*, Vesely gathered, for his own 'collage', an equally impressive and speculative roster of the soon-to-be-famous, including

Tschumi, Koolhaas and Frampton. Reading familiar texts – 'Architecture and its Double', 'Dalí and Le Corbusier: The Paranoid-Critical Method' – in this early context has all the fascination of a primal scene; the scene of a potential reopening of all those tired, reductive grand narratives of architectural Modernism – and the promise of a concomitant reconfiguration of the relations between architecture, utopianism and the avant-garde – at the birth of 'Postmodernism', as well as now at the moment of that (always already) spurious concept's inevitable waning.[2] What might surrealism have contributed to Tschumi's own later definition of architecture as 'the design of conditions that will dislocate the most traditional and regressive aspects of our society and simultaneously reorganize these elements in the most liberating way'? For is it not still the case that 'contemporary architectural trends have obscured – and continue to obscure – the existence of a body of work that contradicts the accepted dogmas of a period' (p 116)?

In one form or another, the emancipatory dream, and the question of its conditions of possibility, runs throughout *Δ* Profile 11 – 'the dilemma of how to be modern', beyond the restricted terms of canonical Modernism's colossal abortions, and with regard to

Image taken from the original *Δ* paper title page.

SURREALISM AND ARCHITECTURE

introduced by Dalibor Veseley:
SURREALISM, MYTH & MODERNITY

I believe in the future resolution of those two seemingly contradictory states, dream and reality, of surreality, to so speak. I look forward to its consummation, certain that I shall never share in it but too indifferent to my death not to taste, at least slightly, the joys of such possession.

(A Breton)[1]

The beauty will be convulsive or will not be at all.

(A Breton)[2]

The real nature of Surrealism, its position and role in modern culture is permanently obscured by the unfortunate identification of the movement with its doctrine, as well as by the no less unfortunate analogies that are made between Surrealism and the established avant-garde (Cubism, Futurism, Dada etc). It is still popular, even today, to believe that Surrealism was, after all, an artistic movement. To anybody who follows carefully its history since the publication of the first Manifesto in 1924, it must soon become clear that this was mainly due to external circumstances – as a response to repeated attacks and criticism, Surrealists had to formulate some of their principles in a way which tends to build a doctrine. It was this merely public face of Surrealism – taken too seriously and uncritically – that made not only so many commentators, and critics, but also a great number of practising Surrealists, blind to the fact that authen-

tic Surrealism is a very different phenomenon.

All the attempts to reduce Surrealism to a set of principles and goals – such as automatism, objective chance, transformation of the world and of life – do not reveal the primary goal of the movement: to reach an absolute point of reconciliation of dream and reality, the

supreme point of all contradictions and to create a completely new reality-surreality, close to the aspirations of the alchemists and their *Grande Oeuvre*.[3]

Seen in that light, Surrealism does not begin in 1919 or 1924, but much earlier, in the romanticism of the 19th century and, to some extent, even earlier in the esoteric and hermetic traditions of the Renaissance. Surrealism does not represent another artistic or political avant-garde, but a subterranean world of the whole modern culture. The dream (and as we will see later, it remained a dream) to complete the surreal *Grande Oeuvre* implies nothing less than total rejection of current logic and culture with all its institutions, total liberation of human desires, and the creation of a world not unlike earthly paradise in which, to use Breton's words

the poet of the future will overcome the depressing idea of an irreparable divorce of action and dream. He will maintain at all costs the common presence of the two terms of

human rapport by whose destruction the most precious conques would become instantaneously worthless: the objective awareness of realities, the internal development in what, by virtue of a sentiment, partly individual, partly universal, is magical until proved otherwise.[4]

On the road to a new myth
In the indefatigable hope expressed in Breton's words that 'not every paradise is lost'[5], the poet is seen as a demiurg (alchemist and magician), who has the power to revolt against the oppressive hegemony of hyperlogical reality, and who is able to create a world which has its own logic – the logic of dreams and the fantastic. The preoccupations of the Surrealists with the marvellous and extraordinary experience – dreams, hallucinations, objective chance and madness – contribute very often to the illusion that Surrealism was only a mosaic of provocative revelations, and, as a whole, was perhaps no more than a semi-rational *methode de recherche*. Underlying what appears on the surface as fragments and unfinished projects, are the esoteric preoccupations of the Surrealists, which were, in fact, much more serious. Apart from their interest in extraordinary every-day phenomena, they have been deeply involved in the study of not only esoteric sciences, but also hermetism, divination and rituals, myths and folklore. Taken together these interests represent the Surrealists' admirable attempt to reconstruct the qualitative universe – 'monde perdu' – forgotten

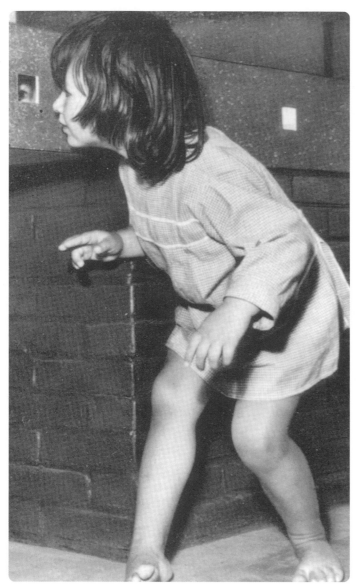

Karin Jaschke has suggested that the work of Van Eyck comes out of a Surrealist architectural thinking on the mytho-poetic as a spatial opening on to a utopian moment.

potential social productions of radical political identities (p 91). For, as Stuart Knight notes in his 'observations', if the surrealists 'dismissed expressionism as being redolent of the "bourgeois love of self"', what they were absolutely not 'prepared to sacrifice' was its 'utopian aspect', its demand for 'the abolition of the "new reality", or its "persecution at least"' (p 102). Hence, as Chris Fawcett suggests, the means by which the likes of Finsterlin and Taut might be 'admitted to the surreal hierarchy by default' (p 126). For us, there is perhaps an entire unwritten history of architectural modernity to be excavated and elaborated from such a remark; one that even the best (Tafuri) have scarcely glimpsed.

For bringing all this into focus, we thus do offer our respect to Dalibor Vesely. Still, we have our misgivings also. Like

Benjamin and Bürger, we balk somewhat at the 'magical-irrationalist' aspect that Vesely privileges – 'hermeticism, divination and rituals, myths and folklore' (p 87) – all that may lead into 'the humid backroom of spiritualism ... with down-at-heel dowagers, retired majors, and émigré profiteers'.[3] For at its worst this results in Peter Smith's witterings about Jung and reactionary speculations that would dissolve the 'differences between contemporary man and his Cro-magnon forebears' in the mists of a 'collective unconscious' (p 151). While, then, Vesely is no doubt right to indicate surrealism's 'romantic precedent', if we are, nonetheless, to resist any contemporary rapprochement with fatuous New Ageisms, it must be understood that the importance of this precedent lies as much in the lure of revolutionary upheaval as in that of mysticism, and leads as much through Marx or Blanqui as through any mythical search for 'primordial links with nature' or 'the return of culture to its archaic origins'[4] (p 91) Basking himself in the glow of surrealism's 'profane illumination', Benjamin writes of that 'inconspicuous spot where in the immediacy of that long forgotten moment the future subsists so eloquently that we, looking back, may rediscover it'.[5] It is by this means that, in the 'now of recognisability', we too might recognise what remains of 'tomorrow' in Vesely's wonderful endeavour.

How then to proceed at this late, and yet still so early, stage? In one of the most admirable contributions to Profile 11, Chris Fawcett, opposing the 'chic surrealism of the shop window', points out that a certain 'surrealism' was apparently 'gaining ground' in Tokyo in the late 1970s by virtue of the fact that advertising was 'becoming a major element of the environment' (p 122). (Fawcett also gives us a delightfully delirious reading of the Smithsons' Robin Hood Gardens as opening a 'gangway to the unconscious'.) Of course, it's a short step from here to what the American poet John Ashbery suggests in a letter to Yippie leader Jerry Rubin, 10 years before the *D* issue (and effectively prefiguring Koolhaas's formula: 'Manhattan = Surreality'): 'President Johnson is a surrealist ... Congress is 95 percent surrealist and ... the entire nation and the world including Vietnam are surrealist places.'[6] Thus, would surrealism, and the faultlines of modernity itself, be reduced to the already given culture of congestion and the 'political complacency of Brandspace', to an ultimate affirmation of the 'irrational' qualities of the new global fluidity of capital flows.[7] Starting in surrealist revolution – albeit in the dissident refrains of Avida Dollars – Koolhaas's 'delirious New York' becomes merely the celebratory prophecy of a 'moment', already emergent in 1978, 'when the logic of media capitalism penetrates the logic of advanced cultural production itself'.[8]

Branded environments: we need the conceptual tools to thoroughly critique the legacy of 19th-century developments through to our own time.

So, on the one hand, there is, then, a classic Tafurian reading of the fate of Profile 11 that must be acknowledged here. Such a reading would be one that traced how the very nature of surrealism's radical possibility – the potential unity of morpho-libidinal and mytho-poetic social spaces – comes inevitably to be closed down, turned into the means of its own failure, as it becomes the latest libidinal tool in capital's commodification of space (and the means by which, as Breton complained, 'experience itself' comes to be 'assigned limits'). Let us not forget that Frederick Kiesler, perhaps the only genuine architect to pass through the movement, found himself as a shop window dresser, grappling with the problems of display as well as risking what Bürger calls the 'false sublation' of art into life.[9] Yet, on the other hand, we might also observe, with Stuart Knight, that 'the fact that consumer commodities still have a "fetishistic" character indicates not a misappropriation of surrealism, and surrealist techniques ... but attests to the survival of the nineteenth-century dream-world into the twentieth-century', in a way that itself demands 'surrealistic' commentary. Knight instances the way in which, for example, the 'architectural fantasies' of Archigram 'display' their 'fetishistic origins' in a manner that is 'almost entirely conditioned by the nineteenth century' (p 103).

As such, it is perhaps most imperative now to understand those aspects of surrealism that conceived of themselves as an extension of an essentially Marxist revolutionary thought (relatively underplayed in the △ issue); a Marxism deluxe that would move beyond the classical/rational 19th-century conceptual models available to Marx himself. Breton suggests

a modern materialist critique, developing tools capable of comprehending and intervening in the interrelated transrational (and increasingly transnational) economies of sex, technology and media. Alas, at the time of Profile 11's publication, even with the sophisticated bodies of Marxist thought then dominant in architectural theory (such as those articulated by Tafuri), the chance to incorporate these practices was still being avoided.

A missed opportunity twice over, then. First, in relation to the received histories of Modernism. Second, in the potential for an adequate critical grasp of architecture's ongoing relation to capitalist development. Is such 'failure' to be always inevitable? Is surrealism's 'haunting' of modernity to be always repressed?[10]

In the company of Dalibor Vesely, we – Jon Goodbun and David Cunningham – along with several others, took it upon ourselves last year to organise the chance meeting of surrealism and architecture in a Manchester lecture hall, with a laudable contempt for what might result in terms of research assessment exercises. We now announce the continuation of this bold enterprise. And we ask this question: For all those supposed 'ends' of this-or-that project of 'modernity' (as if), are we not still living under the reign of logic, albeit those 'irrational' logics of capital itself? And architecture? What of architecture, if it hopes to do more than apply itself only to the solutions of problems of secondary interest? Architecture will be convulsive, or it will not be at all. △

Notes
1 △, Profile 11, Vol 48, No 2–3 (1978). All future references to articles in this issue are given in parentheses in the main body of the text. This essay makes gleeful use of a phraseology and tone borrowed, with an entire absence of credit, from a number of texts, including the first surrealist manifesto of 1924 and Aragon & Breton's 'The Quinquagenary of Hysteria' (1928). Extracts from these can be found in Patrick Waldberg (ed) Surrealism, Thames & Hudson (London), 1965.
2 See David Cunningham, 'Architecture, utopia and the futures of the avant-garde', in David Cunningham, Jon Goodbun and Karin Jaschke (eds) The Journal of Architecture, Special Issue, Post-War Movements, Vol 6, No 2 (Summer 2001), pp 169–82.
3 Walter Benjamin, 'Surrealism: the last snapshot of the European intelligentsia', One Way Street and Other Writings, New Left Books (London), 1979, p 228.
4 See David Cunningham, 'A question of tomorrow: Blanchot, surrealism and the time of the fragment', Papers of Surrealism, No 1 (Winter, 2003): www.surrealismcentre.ac.uk/publications/journal1.htm.
5 Walter Benjamin, 'A small history of photography', One Way Street, op cit, p 243.
6 John Ashbery, 'Growing up surreal', Art News, Vol 67, No 3 (May, 1968).
7 See Jon Goodbun, 'Brand new Tafuri: some timely notes on the imaging of spatial demands', in Cunningham, Goodbun and Jaschke (eds) The Journal of Architecture, op cit, pp 155–68.
8 Frederic Jameson, 'Architecture and the critique of ideology', in K Michael Hays (ed) Architecture Theory Since 1968, MIT Press (Cambridge, MA), 1998, p 456.
9 See Mark Linder, 'Wild kingdom: Frederick Kiesler's display of the avant-garde', in RE Somol (ed) Autonomy and Ideology: Positioning an Avant-Garde in America, Monacelli (New York), 1997, pp 124–53.
10 For some useful comments on the surrealist 'attack' on Corbusian Modernism as 'an attack launched simply enough by revealing that which modernism had repressed', see Anthony Vidler, 'Fantasy, the uncanny and surrealist theories of architecture', Papers of Surrealism, No 1 (Winter, 2003): www.surrealismcentre.ac.uk/publications/journal1.htm. This is the text of a paper delivered at the conference 'Fantasy Space: Surrealism and Architecture', at the Whitworth Art Gallery in Manchester in September 2003, organised by the authors with David Lomas, Gavin Parkinson, Peg Rawes, Anna Dezeuze, Julia Kelly, Dawn Ades. The phrase 'Marxism deluxe' was coined by Karin Jaschke in her paper given at the same event.

SUSTAINING TECHNOLOGY

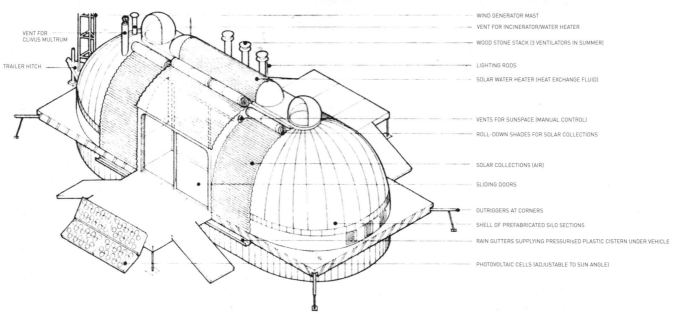

VENT FOR
CLIVUS MULTRUM

TRAILER HITCH

WIND GENERATOR MAST

VENT FOR INCINERATOR/WATER HEATER

WOOD STONE STACK (3 VENTILATORS IN SUMMER)

LIGHTING RODS

SOLAR WATER HEATER (HEAT EXCHANGE FLUID)

VENTS FOR SUNSPACE (MANUAL CONTROL)

ROLL-DOWN SHADES FOR SOLAR COLLECTIONS

SOLAR COLLECTIONS (AIR)

SLIDING DOORS

OUTRIGGERS AT CORNERS

SHELL OF PREFABRICATED SILO SECTIONS

RAIN GUTTERS SUPPLYING PRESSURIsED PLASTIC CISTERN UNDER VEHICLE

PHOTOVOLTAIC CELLS (ADJUSTABLE TO SUN ANGLE)

Early Pioneers, late developers: Survival Capsule (creators unknown), US project, 1970s
This project is bursting with the values of the age – prefabricated and industrialised production of a self-sustaining module. As taken up and more emotively represented later by Future Systems and others, the idea is attractive because it offers users the opportunity to combine the benefits of industrial society with living in the wilderness (while the supporting paraphernalia of society and industrialisation has mysteriously disappeared).

To attempt to capture the extent of the engagement in environmental and ecological issues by architects during the early 1970s as viewed through the pages of ⌀ is an issue in itself. The editorial policy of the magazine at that time was such that it actively commissioned articles and global surveys that would inform the profession of the environmental impact of construction long before 'sustainability' became a convenient buzz word. Robert Webb is one of a new generation of environmental engineers who acknowledges a debt to those who helped to define the terms we use so readily today. He sees how architects fell off the environmental wagon during the middle of the 1970s and are only now beginning to climb back on, but wonders how much understanding of our planet has been lost in the interim.

We asked ourselves the question: Is it possible to grow the food needs of a small group of people in a small space without harming the environment and without enormous recourse to external sources of energy and materials on a continuing basis? The whole idea was: Could we design a system that is self-sustainable and capable of functioning as a system?
— John Todd, New Alchemy Institute, Canada, 1970[1]

This question is relevant to the biggest question of all: the survival of the species. With humankind's influence stretching planetwide, the question suggests we need to better understand the impact we make when we design. Much of the work and theory of the 1970s was occupied with this issue and contains much that we should learn from and be inspired by today.

The age was fascinated with technological advancement, in particular with the development of autonomous buildings and structures that incorporated their own life-support systems – the machine coming alive. The concepts are illustrated by glorious network diagrams exploring flows of energy and resources, while the buildings became increasingly podlike, sprouted wind turbines and sewage treatment plants, and were designed to be delivered complete by helicopter or lorry, arriving in their untouched wilderness sites with minimum impact.

This pioneering work developed mainly through prototypes and unbuilt projects. Here I explore some telling differences between then and now. The abounding technological optimism and resourcefulness of the 1970s was linked to a strong environmental awareness, although based on relatively limited science. Today, in contrast, our scientific knowledge of the environmental crisis is accumulated and detailed, while paradoxically we are dogged and depressed by technological pessimism, and it is unclear whether the political will really exists.

However, a new awareness is emerging: that there is one simple currency that can provide the appropriate value system for a self-sustaining civilisation and technology – energy. This awareness is changing the way buildings are now being designed, and the technologies used to power them.

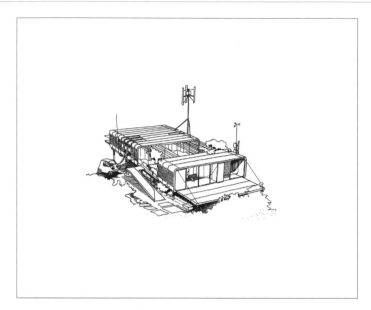

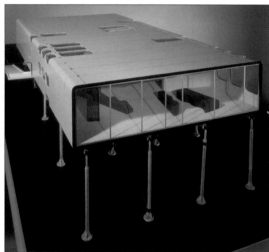

Zip-Up House, Richard Rogers Partnership, 1972
Project using industrial components (refrigerated truck panels)
to create a super-insulated and rapid-deployable housing system.

Technological Optimism

The Cosmorama pages in △ during the 1960s and 70s are full of excitement and passion for the advancing march of technology. The section presents a selection of news clippings from trade journals in construction and science and technology, and newspapers, including a whole column – The Future is Now (FIN) – devoted to listing environmental research bodies around the world.

One short item from an issue in 1971 reports the development of a new way of desalinating water at better efficiencies than before. Another shows the development of LIVE-IN, an instant house made of fibre-glass foam sandwich shell units, for sale in the US for $7,000. A further item reports US attempts to design a pollution-free car, by treating the exhaust fumes. The spirit is evident in other publications of the time: Stewart Brand's *Whole Earth Catalog*[2] provided a compendium of solutions and components for low-impact living. Meanwhile, Victor Papanek's seminal book *Design for the Real World*[3] showed how product design could gain driving inspiration from ethical and environmental issues, overriding ideas of 'brand' and 'image' that were just coming to the fore in design circles.

The Survival Capsule and the Richard Rogers Partnership's Zip-Up House are perfect examples of this technological optimism. The capsule explores optimum physical form for a self-sustaining system, and Zip-Up is a more architectural exploration of the use of manufactured building components. According to Laurie Abbott, senior partner at Richard Rogers Partnership: 'We were using panels from refrigerated trucks, so that the house could be put together in a few days, while also providing fantastic insulation levels – a 1kW heater would keep it happily warm.'[4]

Abbott's comments reveal an interest in generating buildings and products from a first-principles physical understanding of things, following the traditional idea of an architect being a practically minded tinkerer; building wind turbines in the back garden. Today, the profession is dominated by digital and virtual design processes, from drawing to manufacturing, bringing surface to the fore, the inference being that the technology works behind the scenes without directly determining the form making, and that we do not, therefore, need to understand the energy and resource flows: the technology takes care of it out of sight.

The Autarkic House project of Alexander Pike and students at the Martin Centre, University of Cambridge, is another key example that was widely published and has proved influential. The building has a roof-integrated wind turbine for electrical energy production, inter-seasonal heat store for winter heating, and a conservatory for passive solar energy collection and food production. Architectural tourists visiting Cambridge who asked to see it were disappointed to find that the concept was diminutive: the model is 1:10 scale, and funding for a full-scale version was not forthcoming. However, the wind turbine did see further work, and one of its developers, Dr Ian May, is now managing director of wind energy developer Renewable Energy Systems, which builds wind farms all over the world.

Much of the groundwork carried out in the 1970s has contributed to the gradual improvement of building energy regulations and standards, while a series of projects are now moving closer towards the mainstream. Architects Robert and Brenda Vale have built a series of autonomous and low-energy houses in which architecture as art has taken second place to demonstrating that sustainable energy and resource flows can be achieved at low cost, without sacrificing comfort. This work culminated in the Hockerton earth-

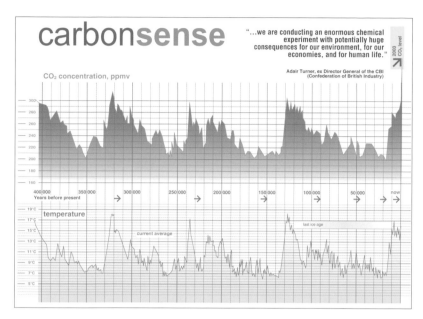

carbonsense

"...we are conducting an enormous chemical experiment with potentially huge consequences for our environment, for our economies, and for human life."

Adair Turner, ex Director General of the CBI (Confederation of British Industry)

CO₂ concentration, ppmv

Years before present

temperature

current average

last ice age

The Need for Carbon-Sense
Graph illustrating the findings from the Vostok ice core. Temperature and CO2 concentrations have been closely in step with each other within a consistent set of values over the last 400,000 years. Current CO2 concentrations are much higher and outside the range.

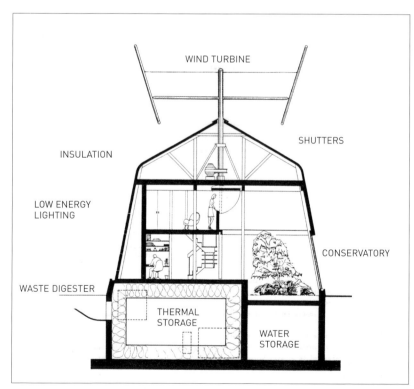

WIND TURBINE

INSULATION

SHUTTERS

LOW ENERGY LIGHTING

CONSERVATORY

WASTE DIGESTER

THERMAL STORAGE

WATER STORAGE

Autarkic House, Alexander Pike and students from the Martin Centre, University of Cambridge, 1972–3
Architectural tourists visiting Cambridge who asked to see the project were disappointed to find that the concept was diminutive: the model is 1:10 scale. Above: Section showing roof-integrated wind turbine for electrical energy production; inter-seasonal heat store for winter heating; conservatory for passive solar energy collection; and plants for food and pleasure. Right: Model on lawn at the Martin Centre.

sheltered and passive solar houses of the late 1990s, where monitoring has confirmed that as long as the buffer space is allowed to be cold in winter, no heating is required. However, Sue Roaf of Oxford Brooks University has argued that ecohouses should look no different from traditional houses; her Oxford Eco-House begins to demonstrate that this can indeed be the case. But there are also others who are using this agenda to explore design innovation.

Environmental Awareness

The *Apollo* programme and moon landing showed architects and artists that they could cocoon and support a human in the most inhospitable of environments – we had the technology and the imagination. But could the house itself be like a spaceship? Stewart Brand spent 1966 making and selling badges that read: 'Why Haven't We Seen A Photograph of the Whole Earth Yet?', urging NASA to make good colour photographs of the earth from distant space – which it eventually did. Meanwhile, the oil crisis of 1973–4 alerted us to the limitations of the key resources that we are so greatly dependent on, speeding up innovation in renewable energy technologies and demonstrating the need for the self-sustainable house.

With such an acute awareness, why then did architecture and commitment to technology falter towards the end of the decade? With the exception of a series of demonstration projects by committed enthusiasts, it wasn't until the 1990s that such issues re-entered mainstream debate, not via architecture, but as a result of the increasing momentum of the environmental lobby.

Scientific confidence in the reality of threats to the environment was relatively undeveloped in the 1970s. The hole in the ozone layer was yet to be discovered and no long-term historical data existed to support the claims of a few scientists as to the possibility of rapid-onset climate change (or global warming).

In contrast, today's scientists are equipped with more of the facts. The graph (above) shows data from ice core samples drilled in Vostok, showing the close relationship between atmospheric CO2 and average temperatures over the past 400,000 years. Current CO2 levels of 370 parts per million are unprecedented in this time frame. Research teams of the International Panel on Climate Change have run approximately 30 different computer simulations. They have predicted as a result that temperatures will rise between 1.5 and 5.8°C over this century, with global mean sea levels rising by 0.9 metres.[5] 'Greenhouse gases are accumulating in the earth's atmosphere as a result of human activities,' says the US National Academy of Sciences, and '... human-induced warming and sea level rises are

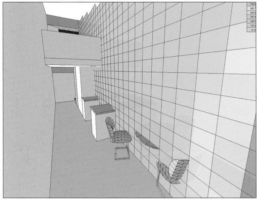

Visualising the Invisible, XCO2, 2003
The invisibles become visible. Computer modelling techniques allowing architecture to be shaped by light, enabling daylighting to be optimised and electrical lighting minimised.

expected to continue throughout the 21st century.'[6] This from an organisation whose current administration has pulled out of the Kyoto Agreement.

Gradual change like this is one thing, but research now also points to rapid-onset climate change as a real possibility, perhaps triggering a new Ice Age. One research group recently calculated the likelihood that by 2065, insurance losses from extreme weather events will reach the same value as total gross domestic product (GDP).

Perhaps the biggest barrier for scientists and designers working in this area in the 1970s was economic theory. The Catch 22 of renewable energy is that the technology required to harness it is not yet produced in large quantities, and therefore tends to be a more expensive initial outlay. The environmentalists' counter-argument to this is that as oil and other resources begin to dry up, their prices will rise, so making non fossil-fuel solutions economic. However, so sceptical of this argument was economist Matthew Simmons that in 1980 he challenged environmentalist Paul Ehrlich to a bet: if the price of a number of key metals went up in a 10-year period, demonstrating the reality of the depletion of nonrenewable resources, then Ehrlich would win the bet. But,

in fact, the prices went down over the period, prompting Simons to claim, bizarrely, that: 'If history is any guide, natural resources will progressively become less costly, hence less scarce.'[7]

Another high-profile attempt to predict the future was made in the 1973 report by the Club of Rome, based on computer modelling of future scenarios and suggesting a catastrophic end to civilisation well before the year 2000.[8] One of the key predictions was that food production would be unable to keep pace with population growth – which has also proved completely unfounded, although an even global distribution is yet to be achieved. The report's claims were extreme and alarmist, and have tended to tar current environmental activists with the same 'daft' brush. Nevertheless, it provided a necessary exercise in imagining unimaginable future scenarios.

However, what we are facing today is the approaching scarcity of our primary fossil fuel – oil – which it is thought has now reached peak production. The current price of around US\$40 per barrel is historically high (due partly to fast-growing demand from China), but not high enough according to energy expert Matthew Simmons at a recent conference on the oil peak: 'The figure I'd use is around \$182 a barrel. We need to price oil realistically to control its demand. That is because global production is peaking.'[9]

Energy is the Machine

We now know that man-made climate change is driven by a basket of greenhouse gases, the most important of which is carbon dioxide. Man-made CO_2 comes from fossil fuels – cars, power stations, houses and factories – and most of it is emitted in order to provide light, heat and power (the 'embodied' or manufacturing energy content of a building is often as low as one-tenth of total lifetime energy).

But progress is probably too slow. The CO_2 reductions in the Kyoto Agreement – an overall 5 per cent reduction by developed countries on 1990 levels by 2010 – will delay climate change by only a few years.

Political action is now being driven by scientific consensus on climate change, leading to international treaties such as the Kyoto Agreement. Progress is being slowed by a few powerful political forces (especially the current US administration), but the treatises will culminate in carbon (or CO_2 emissions-equivalents – CO_2e) becoming a major tradable currency in its own right. The EU emissions trading scheme was due to get under way in January 2005, initially covering major producers such as energy companies and heavy industry. Ultimately, it is likely that each organisation – and perhaps each individual – will have a basic carbon allowance (though they will be able to sell surplus allowances or buy additional), reducing each year with the aim of eventually stabilising climate change.

But progress is probably too slow. The CO_2 reductions in the Kyoto Agreement – an overall 5 per cent reduction by developed countries on 1990 levels by 2010 – will delay climate change by only a few years. UK Prime Minister Tony Blair recently 'made a big speech' on climate change, finally joining the calls for a 'green industrial revolution',[10] but this commitment has not yet become evident in UK government policy, most importantly economic and tax policy where it will

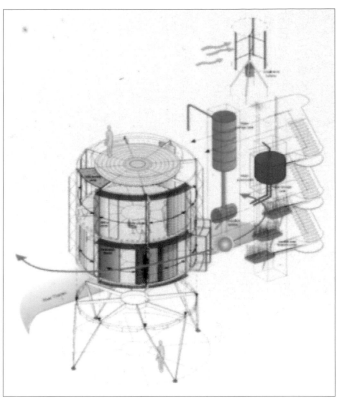

Exhibition building for Renewable Energy in the Urban Environment (RENUE), Robert Webb and Richard Rogers Partnership, London, 1997
Systems and technologies exposed and celebrated, including a water-powered lift. The cylindrical form allows the building to follow the time of day and sun position, while visitors can alter sliding panels, changing the environmental response of the wall construction and directly experiencing the results. A vertical-axis wind turbine, on top of the external stair and service core, produces electrical power.

Humber Centre for Excellence in the Built Environment, Niall McLaughlin Architects and XCO2, Hull, 2004
A modular building that will travel around the city as a focus for discourse about the built environment, moving every three years. An array of small wind turbines and photovoltaic panels showily sway on flexible poles whilst providing total electrical needs. A translucent insulated roof floods the main meeting space with daylight, and waste wood pellets are burnt for winter top-up heat. The building achieves near-zero-carbon performance.

be most influential. Numerous studies by respected institutions[11] have demonstrated that a shift to a low-carbon economy is possible whilst still serving the gods of GDP growth. However, our democratic structures create endemic short-termism, and so perhaps our primary hopes must rest with cultural and social change.

It is clear that our culture needs to internalise a new valuation of energy – electrical energy, heat energy, light energy, air movement, and so on – as first brilliantly intuited in the resource-flow diagrams of the 1970s.

Energy is all. We are still largely unconscious of it, but our entire lives (both urban and rural) are driven by our access to energy (how we use it, why we use it, what sort of energy we use). Access to energy is closely linked to literacy rates in developing countries. Energy is the essential resource enabling the growth of a complex modern civilisation – communication, education, and freeing of the individual from hard labour. And, most critically, it is our current pattern of energy production and consumption that is also its biggest threat.

Architecture and design are now learning to incorporate these factors into the design process, and studios like XCO2 are using complex modelling tools

XCO2 and Solar Century: C21 Solar Tile 2004; Motorway Sound Barrier, M27, Southampton 2003; Solar Canopy, Mile End Park, London 2003–
Photovoltaics (electricity from daylight) developed to seamlessly integrate with today's standard roofing product of choice – the interlocking concrete tile. Meanwhile, the Motorway Sound Barrier offers a less conventional combination of functions. Photovoltaics turns upwards to seek the energy in the sky, while the zig-zag form breaks up sound. The Solar Canopy keeps the rain off, and generates the energy for an electric go-kart track. The clientele are varied: local kids are given an alternative to joy riding, and city gents have the opportunity to find out that electric cars have compelling acceleration.

to understand how buildings can become more responsive to their environments, by applying appropriate technologies. This can be seen most directly in design for light or daylight, where computer design aids the use of new techniques for reflecting and directing light in buildings, or in the prediction of air flow through a building, allowing our buildings to optimise their use of ambient resources, minimising reliance on fossil-fuelled technology black boxes.

But there is a very real danger of tokenism. Since very few people understand even the basic principles of energy use, it is easy for developers and architects to mouth the right words while delivering no actual improvement. Lack of clarity in public standards and targets is also hugely counterproductive; at the time of writing, it is relatively easy to gain a high rating in the Building Research Establishment (BRE) EcoHomes scheme, which also massively undervalues the single most important issue – energy. So we are still relying on the commitment and honesty of a few pioneers to deliver real environmental project improvements.

On a more positive note, a growing number of projects have overtly taken inspiration from the energy agenda. The proposed Solar Canopy (in the East End of London) uses solar energy to define its geometry. Photovoltaic cells (generating electricity from daylight) clad south-facing facades of the supporting arches in the adaptation of a historic form (sawtooth roof) to a new problem: keeping the rain off whilst at the same time generating the energy for an electric go-kart racing track, with surplus to spare.

Another key energy resource is the wind, harvesting of which is a highly developed and cost-effective technology. Wind on buildings provides particularly fertile opportunities, as there are no transmission losses and the form of the building can be exploited to increase energy, as demonstrated by XCO2's Living Towers concept and 'quiet rEvolution' design for a vertical-axis wind turbine that is optimised for constant driving force with minimum vibration and noise, and capable of taking advantage of turbulent winds.

In addition, the Humber Centre for Excellence in the Built Environment, by Niall McLaughlin Architects with XCO2 (on site at the time of writing), aims to achieve zero-carbon performance through an array of small wind turbines and solar panels in a sculptural 'energy thicket', a wood-pellet burning boiler for heat, and a high-performance translucent roof engineered for an optimum balance between heat loss and daylight – the whole forming an entertaining and elegant exhibition of some of the key technology and design solutions now available to us.

Such approaches – of architecture formed by energy awareness – are being applied by more and more designers, in urban designs to buildings and products, some of which are being built today in full-size working versions, not just 1:10 models. While much of the mainstream pays only lip service to energy issues, the word is spreading, albeit slowly, for a culture change that makes the previously invisible energy a cornerstone of our design awareness. ☎

Notes
1 John Todd, in Chris Zelov (ed) *Design Outlaws on the Ecological Frontier*, Knossus Publishing (Philadelphia PA), 1997.
2 Published annually by Stewart Brand from 1968 to 1974.
3 Victor Papanek, *Design for the Real World*, Thames and Hudson (London), 1985.
4 Discussion with the author.
5 IPCC 'Third Assessment Report: Climate Change', July 2001, www.ipcc.ch.
6 Report to the Bush administration, June 2001.
7 BBC Online, http://news.bbc.co.uk/1/hi/business/3777413.stm.
8 Donna H Meadows et al, *The Limits to Growth: A Report for the Club of Rome's Project on the Predicament of Mankind*, Pan Macmillan (London), 1974.
9 BBC Online, http://news.bbc.co.uk/1/hi/business/3777413.stm, 7 June 2001.
10 http://news.bbc.co.uk/1/hi/uk_politics/3656812.stm, 4 September 2004.
11 For example, see Paul Ekins, 'The UK's Transition to a Low-Carbon Economy', policy briefing PB5 by Forum for the Future, June 2001.

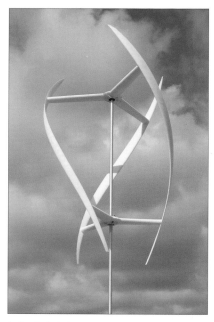

'quiet rEvolution' vertical-axis wind turbine, XCO2, 2004
Prototype: the dreams of the 1970s are now becoming real. The geometry of the turbine is driven by aerodynamic engineering created by mathematical algorithms to maximise both performance and elegance.

Zero-Carbon Living Towers, XCO2, 2004
Research project to demonstrate a practical approach to integrate accelerated wind energy into the built environment. The aerofoil form of the towers drives wind through the turbines at typically double normal speed, enabling the turbines to produce the entire energy needs of the apartment's inhabitants.

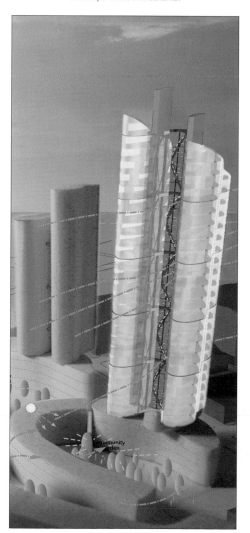

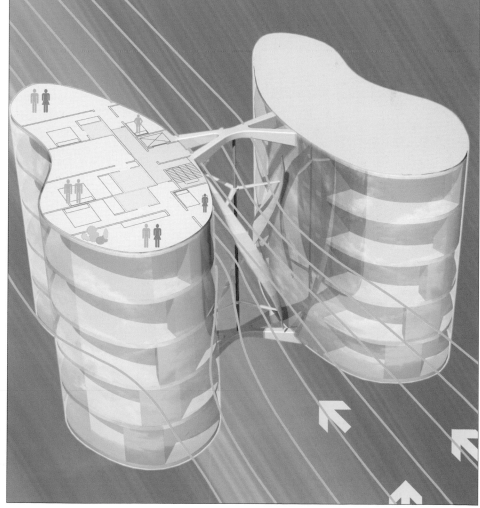

HMMMM GARDENING...
SOME COMMENTS ON GARDEN STYLE & FALSE ECONOMY

Architects beware! Seized with your renewed vigour for 'greening' your schemes, you must know that there are plants, and there are plants, and that they should not be misinterpreted. Jon Vincent has strong opinions about how divisive some landscaping decisions can become, and incorporates these rules into his own, more responsive, garden designs.

These well-managed Leylandii overshadow an intriguing rockery.

Consumed by conifers, these monsters were probably planted as ornamental miniatures 30 years ago.

X Cupressocyparis Leylandii

photographed by Angus Mill

hmmmmm....

Example of the plant labels used at the 2004 RHS Malvern Spring
Gardening Show, Worcestershire, UK.

The Wedge-Hedge An Urban Style Show Garden for the Malvern Spring Gardening Show 2004

Viewed from two sides this beautifully stark, minimal garden is full of conflict and cotridiction. Immaculately clipped ivy, buxus, yew and beech hedges juxtapose a brutally pruned line of mature Leylandii trees. Mounted in the tops of the tree stumps is an LED display showing a moving text stating the present Leylandii laws.
Lush turf, tiered hedging, LED displays and passing crowds will lend a sporting atmosphere to the contentious issues of personal borders, anti-social planting and physical boundaries.

This proposal for a show garden was accepted for the 2004 Malvern
Spring Gardening Show. The public response to the garden when built
was fascinating to observe.

The buxus wedge hedge is the Flora Gardens trademark. It is a sculptural planting that adds structure and style to any garden.

The garden at Malvern showcased the 'cutting hedge' style of Flora Gardens, including the trademark wedge hedge. In this instance, the sculptural buxus wedge hedge was planted as a symbol of the divide that occurs when a Leylandii hedge gets between neighbours.

In the same way as our homes slowly fill with oversized, dysfunctional furniture, unwanted gifts, bric-a-brac and general clutter, our gardens, too, are full of misplaced plants, pots and trees that are just too big to move.

Contrary to popular belief, the garden is not an outside room. There might be parallels drawn between vacuuming the carpet and mowing the lawn, but here the comparisons should end. The great outdoors is an exciting, ever-changing environment that now, more than ever, is quite unpredictable. The weather can be harsh and unforgiving. Airborne disease is rife and animal invasion is always a threat.

Much more predictable, though, is our insatiable appetite for hideous plants, such as Busy Lizzies, Fuschias, Photenias, Robinias, Leylandii etc. All too available at a garden centre near you. Sometimes the weather is not harsh enough for these eyesores and, along with state-of-the-art growing techniques that don't even involve the outdoor environment, these plants are everywhere. The only way to curb this tendency and cull these fast-growing favourites is simple economics based on supply and demand. We do not really demand these plants, they just happen to be cheaply available at the drive-in superstore. Without much thought they are purchased, plonked in the ground and, because they grow, that must be a good thing.

Is *Cupressocyparis leylandii* a good thing? A household favourite of the 1970s, it is still very popular today – as I discovered at the 2004 RHS Malvern Spring Gardening Show. Flora Gardens entered a show garden inspired by the debate

surrounding the proposed High Hedges Bill; the idea that planting Leylandii hedges could be deemed antisocial behaviour and that you might be incriminated for a random act of gardening is a fascinating one.

The garden at Malvern showcased the 'cutting hedge' style of Flora Gardens, including the trademark wedge hedge. In this instance, the sculptural buxus wedge hedge was planted as a symbol of the divide that occurs when a Leylandii hedge gets between neighbours. Brutally pruned tree stumps suggested a recently resolved dispute and acted as mounts for electronic LED screens that headlined the main points of the new legislation governing antisocial hedges. Oversized plant labels hung from newly planted Leylandii saplings with photographic examples of mismanaged Leylandii.

Alternative planting suggestions were to be found on the reverse of the labels. Around 95,000 people attended the Malvern Show, and it was exciting to see the mixed reaction to the garden with its underlying messages. There was a lot of support for the new legislation, which will give local authorities the power to order 2-metre-high pruning of offending antisocial hedges. Passionate, was the defence of well-managed, clipped Leylandii hedges. Critical, were those supporters of the bad press that Leylandii receives. Castlewellan Gold variety is a particular favourite and apparently an important habitat for wildlife.

Frustratingly, the Flora Gardens exhibit at Malvern did not have enough floral content to be judged as an RHS show garden. This is ironic, because it was making a statement about plant selection, suggesting that one should be more discerning in one's choice of plants, that we should look to the classics such as box, beech, hornbeam, oak and yew, and encourage the use of these traditional favourites in imaginative new ways instead of the predictable use of cheap garden centre stock. There is no place for 'cheap and cheerful'. Look where it has got us with quick-fix Leylandii. Plant plonking is unacceptable. It is here that we can assert consumer control and ignore bargain buys and simply refuse to purchase ugly plants. ◮

ACTIVE NARRATIVES

The archive at the Fonds Régional d'Art Contemporain du Centre (FRAC Centre), Orléans, France, houses an outstanding collection of experimental architectural models and drawings from the 1950s, 1960s and 1970s. Marie-Ange Brayer has worked closely with the archive for many years and is now its director. Here, she draws out some examples from the collection to describe how the emergence of 'narrative' in 1960s and 1970s Europe, and then in the US, transformed the architectural project from the singular representation of form into a multidimensional shared script for action.

Rem Koolhaas (with Madelon Vriesendorp and Elia Zenghelis), *The City of the Captive Globe*, 1972
Acrylic paint, gouache on paper, 31 x 44 centimetres
Photograph: Olivier Martin-Gambier
Within the archipelago of blocks, the terrestrial globe is in a state of incubation. Each block contains an idea, or an artistic discipline, which is developed through mutant architectural forms in the midst of many different references, ranging from Le Corbusier to Malevich.

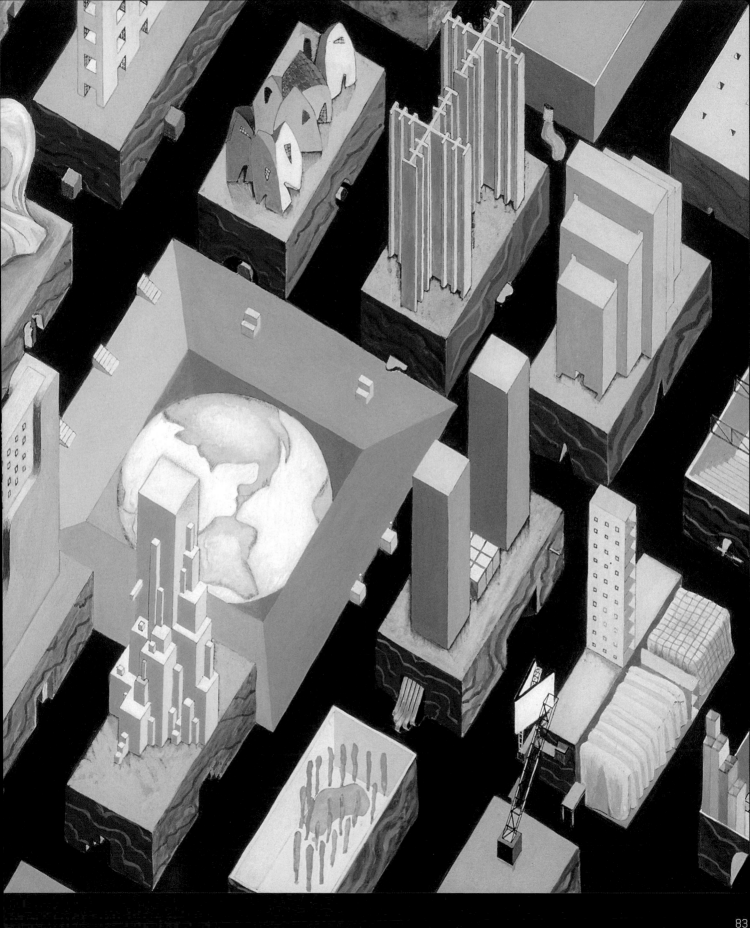

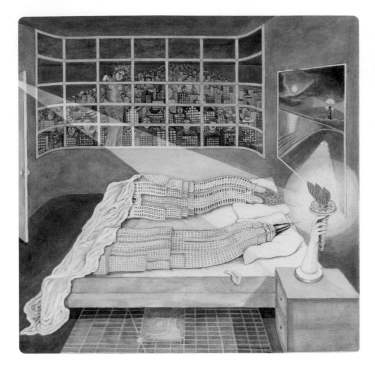

Rem Koolhaas (with Madelon Vriesendorp and Elia Zenghelis), *Flagrant délit*, 1975
Watercolour and gouache on paper, 35 x 40 centimetres
Photograph: Olivier Martin-Gambier
In an at-once Surrealist and Pop atmosphere, *Flagrant délit* – a transcription of
'Manhattanism' and the 'culture of congestion'– displays the grid as urban unconsciousness.
Here, the city delivers its mechanistic unconsciousness and the many skyscrapers are like so
many 'desirous machines'.

Franco Raggi, *La Tenda rossa*, 1975
Paint on canvas and wood, 275 x 290 x 350 centimetres
Copyright: Palazzo delle Papesse, Siena
As nomadic architecture, the Red Tent is a paradoxical object. As an unusual merging
of the ancient Vitruvian temple and the primitive cabin-hut, as theorised by Laugier in
the 18th century, it deconstructs the myth of the origin of architecture.

For centuries, architectural output was subjected to the theory of imitation, and part and parcel of the normative framework of the 'model'. However, at the end of the 18th century this framework was to crack as a result of the autonomisation of the architectural project, as illustrated, for example, by Piranesi's architectural 'heterotopias', as Tafuri called them. Piranesi transformed the architectural order into a maze of spatial narratives, distorting, reducing and breaking down space. In this respect, Tafuri underscored the systematic criticism of the concept of place in Piranesi's work, where space breaks up into heterogeneous particles that no longer put any pre-established order back together (*Carceri d'invenzione; Campo Marzio*, 1761–2).

Much later on, the modern avant-gardes of the early 20th century radicalised this project-related autonomy, freeing architecture from its constructive purpose. The postwar period, in turn, created a crisis in the notion of norm and model. The iconoclastic 'radical' architects of the 1960s and 1970s in Europe resorted to provocation and paradox, and did battle with the very identity of architecture, challenging its language and pushing Modernism back against the wall. The project's form thus freed itself from the rule and the model, and became an instrument of confrontation with society. In this desire to demystify the language of architecture, representation was toppled, and new narrative forms emerged, turning the project into a 'heterotopia', into a plural and multidimensional place.

Once divorced from the diktat of representation, the narrative that was ushered in combined with action, seeking to appropriate the complexity of the real. It was no longer form that mattered, but the use made of it. Architecture thus asserted itself as an artistic, not to say conceptual praxis.

In many late-1960s and early-1970s projects, the project turned into the convergence of a proliferation of narrative topoi, making architectural production attributable. This narrative heterogeneity adopted several referential chords: recourse to science fiction and the world of comic strips peculiar to the Anglo-Saxon culture, as illustrated by the Archigram projects, which for the first time 'serialised' the architectural image; and the incorporation of geographical maps within the project, turning it into heterogeneous narrative territory, a novel collage of abstraction and reality, as in the works of Superstudio. This territorial extension of the image of the architectural project was accentuated in the artistic context of Land Art and Conceptual Art, the influence of which would be felt in Gianni Pettena's performances and James Wines's interventions in the early 1970s.

The normative dimension of the model thus gave way to narrative action within productions using heterogeneous media, aimed at linking up with the very contingency of the real, which we shall now explore, using one or two significant examples.

Rem Koolhaas: Delirious New York (1972–8), Or the Originless Narrative of Architecture

After his early days influenced by Situationism, and as a scriptwriter to boot, Rem Koolhaas produced several theoretical projects with Elia and Zoe Zenghelis and Madelon Vriesendorp: in 1970, *The Berlin Wall as Architecture*, and in 1972, *Exodus or: the voluntary prisoners of architecture*. From 1973 to 1976, living mainly in New York, he began writing the book that

Franco Raggi, *Scala con Villa*, 1975
Pastels on paper, 36.5 x 25.5 centimetres
Photograph: Philippe Magnon
As the cover illustration for *Casabella* magazine, 'Scala con Villa' is part of Franco Raggi's series of 'unstable architectures', brimming with paradox and irony, and questioning the language of architecture.

UFO (Lapo Binazzi), *Projet pour l'Université de Florence*, 1974
Retouched pastels, 50 x 70 centimetres
Photograph: Philippe Magnon
As part of the Manifesto of Discontinuity, Lapo Binazzi breaks down the architectural order in his drawings with their mix of references from popular culture and the media, as well as the electrifying figure of Mao Zedong growing cabbages near the Great Wall of China.

would analyse the impact of metropolitan culture on architecture. *Delirious New York: A Retroactive Manifesto for Manhattan* was published in 1978 in New York, London and Paris, and was to have a marked effect on all subsequent generations of architects.

As an archipelago of blocks, *The City of the Captive Globe* (1972) illustrated this Manhattanesque culture of congestion. In the middle, the terrestrial globe was in a state of incubation, rising up in time with the development of ideas, with each block forming the pedestal. 'Each Science or mania has its own plot ... From these solid blocks of granite, each philosophy has the right to expand indefinitely toward heaven ... The collapse of one of the towers can mean two things: failure, giving up, or a visual Eureka, a speculative ejaculation.'[1]

Littered with allusions to the grid of Le Corbusier's *Plan Voisin*, and with the Suprematist theories of Malevich's 'architektones', *The City of the Captive Globe* was a pure mental construct dominated by the endless repetition of the grid absorbing all manner of urbanism, and thus guaranteeing the immutability of the system. This systematism of the grid also referred to Superstudio's *Histogrammes* (1969), three-dimensional diagrams extending ad infinitum, consuming the disappearance of scale between architecture, furniture and urbanism. Nevertheless, while Superstudio's grid kept its abstraction intact, heir to Hilberseimer and Neurath, in *Delirious New York* Koolhaas turned it into a patchwork of heterogeneous narratives, effecting the disappearance of the architectural place. Here, the city became fiction, a fantasy narrative, where dream and reality emulsified with a heterogeneous corpus of references.

Flagrant délit (1975), for its part, borrowed its dreamlike imagination from the Surrealist legacy, as well as from Pop Art. Once again, fantastic narratives coexisted with fragments of reality, informed by the mutant and symbiotic body of the metropolis. The city delivered its mechanistic unconscious, and in it skyscrapers were like so many 'desirous machines'.

Flagrant délit conjures up for us the textual fragmentations of Allen Ginsberg about the city, and William Burroughs in *The Naked Lunch*. Its iconography likewise subscribed to the Freudian mechanisms of the dream, operating by way of displacement and condensation. In this night-time scene, two skyscrapers are surprised in bed. Outside, 'peeping-tom' skyscrapers conjure up Salvador Dalí's 'paranoid-critical conquest'.

The work is an anamnesis of architecture, proceeding by way of conglomerates of local and disjunctive memories, echoing the 'blocks' which, by being congregated, form the urban archipelago. For Koolhaas, the architect comes across as manipulated by the forces of the subconscious element of a culture. Manhattanism is here described as a 'technology of fantasy', whose transformations comply with the rules of psychic life. In the mid-1970s, the narrative processes applied by *Delirious New York* profoundly jolted the nature of the architectural project by making it implode as fragmented narrative instances, no longer leading to the uniqueness of the project, but endlessly promoting its dislocation.

Radical Italy: Architecture As 'Narrative Action'
In Italy in the 1970s, *Casabella* magazine, edited by Alessandro Mendini, played the role of nothing less than an intellectual arena for radical architecture, championed by Ettore Sottsass Jr, Superstudio, and Archizoom. The year 1973 saw the founding in Italy of Global Tools, an alternative design school, the purpose of which was to stimulate individual creativity. One famous contributor to *Casabella*, who at the time designed many of the magazine's covers, was Franco Raggi – architect, critic and designer – who endeavoured to dissect and analyse the conventions of architectural language. So *La Tenda rossa* (1974–5)

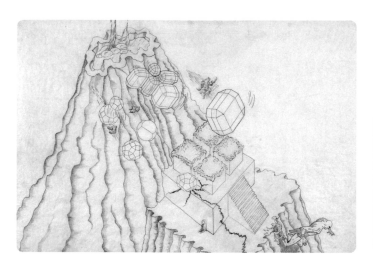

UFO (Lapo Binazzi), *Projet de ville sous le cratère*, 1970
Crayon on paper, 69.5 x 91 centimetres
Photograph: Philippe Magnon
As an iconoclastic supporter of urban guerilla tactics, Binazzi plonks a Greek temple in a mountain landscape, while Spiderman tries to escape from a spray of stones spat out by an erupting volcano. Architecture is henceforth liable to the assaults of chaos and irrationality.

Gianni Pettena, *Ice House II, Minneapolis,* Etats-Unis, 1972
Original colour print, 31 x 40 centimetres
Photograph: Philippe Magnon
In *Ice House II*, Minneapolis, Pettena developed a wooden device, over which he poured water, thus imprisoning a suburban house in an ice cube. Pettena's interventions lie at the crossroads of Conceptual Art and Land Art, exploring the relationship between nature and architecture.

literally deconstructed the notion of the model in architecture, while at the same time paying no heed to codes and references. *The Tent* was built and hand-painted by Raggi using traditional techniques, making it a paradoxical object, difficult to situate, at once maquette and prototype, an unusual mixture of the ancient Vitruvian temple and the primitive cabin-hut, as theorised by Abbot Laugier in the 18th century. Its branches are intertwined with the representation of the pediment of a Greek temple and a colonnade.

The Tent ushered a visual and temporal ambiguity into the rationalist systems it challenged. It mockingly questions those origins of architecture that for centuries nurtured architectural criticism. In its ironical questioning of architectural language, it thus steps up the number of narrative styles. Raggi was possibly also referring to the statement made by Boullée, for whom architecture was above all a 'production of images'. The myth of the primitive cabin, revisited using antiquity as a yardstick, disintegrates in the contingency of the artistic, pictorial gesture, and in the fragility of a fabric construction that runs counter to the claimed permanence and fixedness of architecture. The archetype has here become contingent by way of the introduction of narrative mainsprings that are forever activating paradoxical references, and contradicting the presumed transcendence of architecture.

In Florence, in this same iconoclastic chord, UFO (1967–78) deconstructed the narrative conventions of architectural representation through performances, urban guerrilla actions, and images borrowed from Pop culture. With the condition of alienation engendered by capitalism, it was the intent of UFO to replace creative behaviour and liberation by imagination. By blurring the distinction between furniture and décor, it created one of the first examples of 'narrative architecture' with the *Sherwood Restaurant* (1969).

As part of the Manifesto of Discontinuity the same year, UFO, together with Lapo Binazzi, sought to draw closer to the architecture of the visual arts by way of a series of drawings breaking down the architectural order, mingled with references from popular culture and the media, from the figure of Mao Zedong cultivating cabbages near the Great Wall of China, to Spiderman. Binazzi's incredible pencil drawings thus juxtaposed the plan of a Greek Temple, with its elevation, perched on a mountain, smashed by a spray of enormous stones spat by an erupting volcano, from which Spiderman is trying to flee as fast as he can! Architecture formally governed by rules is henceforward liable to the assaults of chaos and irrationality. Here, architecture as representation and model is literally pulverised with a scathing irony, taken up by UFO in its theory of 'discontinuity', a juxtaposition of heterogeneous, semantic, textual and visual fragments, hampering any grasp of it as a whole, an organic uniqueness, the architectural project. Discontinuity here permits the coexistence of several narrative actions, within which the creative process finds its singularity.

In the radical movement, Gianni Pettena came across both as an artist, using the language of architecture, and as an architect appropriating systems of artistic logic. His experimental work in the 1970s lies at the crossroads of Conceptual Art and Land Art, forever exploring the relationship between nature and architecture. In 1971, in Minneapolis, with *Ice House I*, Pettena poured water along the old administrative premises of a school during the night. The building froze, and was entirely covered with a translucent layer of ice. Like Gordon Matta-Clark, Pettena was involved in an 'act

James Wines and SITE, *Indeterminate Façade*, Best Showroom, Houston, 1975
Cardboard, plastic, Plexiglas, plaster, wood, paint, paper, glue, 20 x 91 x 90.5 centimetres
Photograph: Philippe Magnon
Indeterminate Façade seems suspended between construction and demolition. A cascade of bricks unfurls from the walls and invades the public space of the street: a building in ruins, or construction in progress? James Wines challenges the principle of indeterminacy at the heart of architecture.

of displacement' in which architecture reverted to its raw and physical matter. Living in everything was thus rendered impossible, and space was irrevocably deconstructed (in this respect, James Wines would see in Pettena a forerunner of the deconstruction of the 1980s). In *Ice House II*, Pettena developed a wooden device over which he once again poured water, which in turn imprisoned a suburban house in a cube of ice. The intent behind the Ice House pieces was to inoculate architecture with the immanence and temporality of nature, triggering a new narrative form within the architectural process.

James Wines/SITE: Architecture or Narrative Ambiguity

For James Wines, architecture is likewise experienced in its developing and indeterminate dimension. In the 1970s, SITE achieved international recognition with works such as *Indeterminate Façade* (Houston, 1975), and Inside/Outside Building (Milwaukee, 1984), with their unfinished brick facades for the large Best stores. *Indeterminate Façade* seems to be suspended between construction and demolition, in a temporal indecisiveness. A cascade of bricks tumbles from the wall and invades the public space of the street. Passers-by thenceforth saw themselves involved in a direct confrontation with the building: building in ruins or construction in progress? In the Best stores, the 'building is changed very little physically, but a whole lot psychologically',[2] to use Wines's words. This challenging ambiguity also conjures up the contemporary

theories of Robert Venturi, from *Complexity and Contradiction in Architecture* (1966), to *Learning from Las Vegas* (1977) and the 'decorated shed' notion where the facade is separated from the rest of the architecture, as in the Best stores.

Popular culture, which had impregnated Pop Art, and the critical essays of Charles Jencks – then marked by the impact of signs and metaphors – both had an influence on Wines's projects, as did Karl Jung's analysis of the logic of dreams. Wines's architecture proceeds by dissociation and fragmentation, summoning the irrational and the ambiguous. In the first of his buildings to be constructed (*Indeterminate Façade*, Houston), he drew from the imagery of advertising, sitcoms, rock music and the junk culture, as well as from the huge diversity and heterogeneity of that contextual world usually rejected by architecture.

For Wines, 'the context is the content', and he saw in this Best store 'the first architectural equivalent of an assisted readymade',[3] or an iconographic statement based on the indeterminacy that hallmarks all production, be it artistic, visual, acoustic or architectural. For the form is no longer a means of becoming acquainted with architecture, dissolved in its many faceted and ever-moving context – the context of a narrative forever being updated in present time. Inclusion, dissociation, and chance can now be asserted as operational principles of architecture, which, thanks to them, regains its original status of public artwork. Architecture here focuses on a new principle of individuation, through the flows of a narrative dimension that enable it to sidestep the peremptory character of form.

This new significance of narrative as a device of fragmentation and action on the real, permeated the 1970s, deeply altering the status of the architectural work of the time, as well as that of the author: in effect, the production of these 'images', with their ambiguous status, transformed the architectural project into a shared scenario based on individual appropriation. As with Walter Benjamin, who used the metaphor of the 'narrator' to define the creative artist's stance, the architect is here positioned as 'narrator' and, accordingly, permits an 'exchange of experiences'. These new architectural narratives thus usher us into the territory as an act of experience, activating intersubjectivity to the detriment of the approach that is introspective and devoid of form. Architecture therefore emerges, in these projects and works, like an active narrative, grappling with reality as much as with imagination. ∆

Notes
1 Rem Koolhaas, *Delirious New York: A Retrospective Manifesto for Manhattan*, Monacelli Press (New York), 2002.
2 James Wines, *De-Architecture*, Rizzoli (New York), 1987, p 145.
3 Wines, op cit.

THINKO

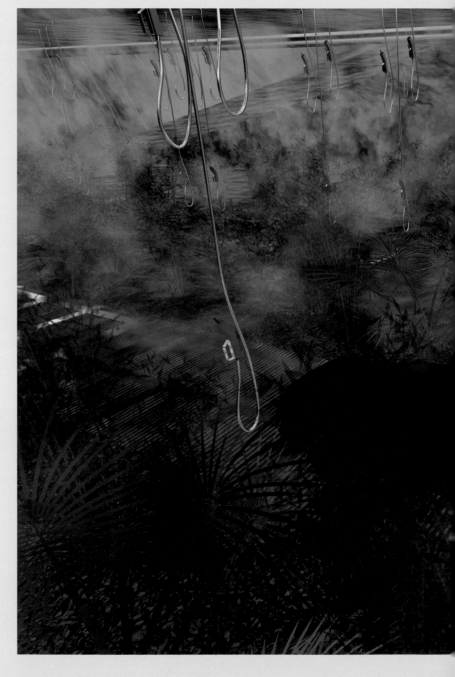

THINKORAMA is a special section devised for this issue dedicated to ideas, thinking about ideas, writing about and making ideas. Full credit for the title must go to champion and first lady of architectural ideas, director of the Canadian Centre for Architecture, Phyllis Lambert, who coined the phrase on the eve of a presentation of Cedric Price's 'Potteries Thinkbelt' in November 2003 at the University of Westminster. The event, called 'SuperCrit', was endorsed by Price, but his untimely death in the summer of that year prevented him from presenting the project himself. It was therefore handed to a group of friends and associates to argue the profundity of this great architectural work-on-paper. As for **NOW** ... Price would have us remember, it is up to all to keep on thinking.

RAMA

1. The Smart Park

The Smart Park is a drive-through, covered hydrogen-refuelling park along the Westway in central London that anticipates a better transport policy 20 years into the future. Inside the park, motorists can enjoy scenic landscapes and a tropical climate whilst filling up their hydrogen-powered cars. It provides a working ecosystem for the car and the road, converging the organic and the mechanical in order to create an environmentally friendly strategy. Duckweed is grown, and mulched down to produce methane gas, the latter then being chemically separated to form hydrogen. The duckweed is heated to accelerate the mulching process, producing excess heat in the chambers that permeates up through the building and creates a microclimate suitable for tropical plants. A natural cycle of fuel consumption is created, and an elevated section of motorway is transformed into an oasis in the city.
— Marion Clayfield

2. '£5,000,000 Worth Of Prizes to be Won in the Weetabix Virtual Games. Has Your Athlete Got the Energy to Win?'

Virtual Games. Has your athlete got the energy to win?

Your competitor number is printed on the inside of this packet and a virtual athlete is online ready and waiting to race for you. Log on to www.weetabixgames.co.uk and enter your number, and let your athlete join the line-up. If they've got the energy to take Gold, Silver, Bronze or 4th place, then you win a prize. In celebration of the 5 Olympic rings, there are 5 Prize Camps to choose from, so you'll be spoilt for choice! For a closer look, log on! Ready to race? Race to win!' ©Weetabix Ltd
— Maggie Smith

3. Don't (Bother To) Cut the Grass

this vegetation is not being cut for environmental reasons

THANK YOU FOR YOUR SUPPORT
Ballyliffin Residents' Association

The village of Ballyliffin regularly achieves a respectable score in the annual 'Tidy Town's Competition', a nationwide contest across the Republic of Ireland. But there is room for improvement in the 'Landscaping' category, and much room for improvement in the section for 'Wildlife and Natural Amenities'. With a resident population of 850, of which less than 1 per cent are actively involved, the Ballyliffin Residents' Association (BRA) has real problems garnering the necessary support to achieve a higher score. So the BRA erect signs that attempt to absolve them from maintenance in the name of environmental responsibility. They subvert how the place is viewed, and thus what is seen.
— Gary Doherty with Petra Marguc

4. Play Walk One, Or 3 Acts in 117 Signs

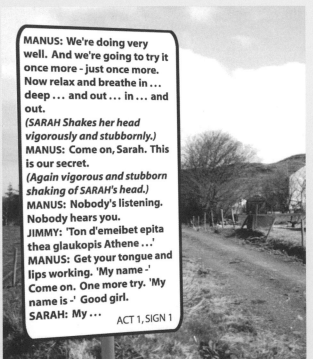

MANUS: We're doing very well. And we're going to try it once more - just once more. Now relax and breathe in ... deep ... and out ... in ... and out.
(SARAH Shakes her head vigorously and stubbornly.)
MANUS: Come on, Sarah. This is our secret.
(Again vigorous and stubborn shaking of SARAH's head.)
MANUS: Nobody's listening. Nobody hears you.
JIMMY: 'Ton d'emeibet epita thea glaukopis Athene ...'
MANUS: Get your tongue and lips working. 'My name -' Come on. One more try. 'My name is -' Good girl.
SARAH: My ...

ACT 1, SIGN 1

Can landscape animate text as well as text animate landscape? Can they help interpret each other? The entire text of Irish playwright Brian Friel's *Translations* is to be placed on signs along 6.2 kilometres of footpaths in three locations, or acts. Instead of scenes, there are 117 signs, each 300 x 560 millimetres, erected on poles 50 metres apart. The ubiquitous road-signs reflect an accepted roadside aesthetic and hints of a cheeky improvisation inherent in Friel's work. Each is an epiphany of sorts, and reminds us of the old local practice of the *turas* (annual pilgrimage, or journey, to holy wells, with prayers recited along the way).
— Gary Doherty with Raoul Bunschoten

5. Suburban House Kit

For $75 per square foot, Adam Kalkin will build you the house of your dreams from five recycled-steel shipping containers. For an extra $1,000, the architect will cook you dinner in your new home himself. Suburban House Kit was exhibited in 2004 at New York City's Deitch Projects. It is a 2,000-square-foot, two-storey prefabricated Quik House ('Quik satisfaction guaranteed!'), available in four floor plans, with an additional four roof choices, including a roof deck with solar curtain or a lush turf deck. Kalkin and his international group of collaborators were selling not only the shell of a house, but a complete customisable living environment, with options including a video installation by Aernout Mik, an origami garden by Tobias Rehberger, a Viking stainless steel fireplace/kitchen module, a slick red Nissan Infiniti G35 in the driveway, and a second-floor library stocked with 1,000 copies of Kalkin and Mik's book *Addiction*. An ambiguous consumable environment was created that was at once cosy, frightening and, finally, too strange to be livable. However, stripped of its status as art object, the Quik House has a life beyond the gallery. Its beauty lies in its utility, affordability and lightening-fast time-to-complete – certain to delight even the most impatient and addicted 21st-century consumers.
— Annalise Reed

6. Living With Interactive Architecture

Nothing I am going to say here is new to the field of architecture from a general conceptual standpoint, and yet it still keeps me up at night. Interactive architecture finally seems to have arrived. Interactive systems are conceptually realistic, technically possible and economically feasible. Such systems introduce a new approach to architectural design where objects are conventionally static, use is often singular, and responsive adaptability is typically unexplored. The development of interactive architecture requires the use of advanced computational design tools, kinetic engineering and embedded computation (including sensor technology and software development), and an ever-unfolding knowledge of new materials. Application design comes from architects learning to make convincing extrapolations based on where we stand today through inclusively appreciating and marshalling the existing facts with respect to technological development. Exacerbating this task is the foolishness to name what we are experiencing in terms of general technological advance as a revolution; it is an evolution, to which an end cannot be predicted outside the parameters of political, commercial and economical entanglement. The clear motivation here lies in creating spaces and objects that can physically reconfigure themselves to meet changing needs. Interactive systems arise from the isomorphic convergence of embedded computational infrastructures (intelligence) and the physical mechanisms that satisfy the needs (kinetics) as situated within the contextual framework of human and environmental interaction (the changes). Interactive architectural systems can serve as a means for inventing entirely new ways of developing spaces, and the designing and building environments that address dynamic, flexible and constantly changing needs. An intelligent car today can clearly understand who is using it and adapt to the personal preferences of that particular driver, whilst at the same time handling issues of automated navigation, safety and security. Embedded computation is becoming more simplified, affordable and, therefore, commercially accessible. Architects need to take a more active role in directing the development of this area of design. For in order to extrapolate the existing conditions of a computationally integrated architecture into a vision of the future is a conundrum residing in the hands of architects and designers directing the future of their profession. In learning to think how an architectural environment can be empowered to adapt that goes beyond a mere capacity to adapt. Designers need to think of adaptive response to change as creating objects and spaces that can intelligently moderate both human activity and the environment. This is a new way of thinking about space from a pragmatic and tectonic standpoint, yet it seems very obvious from a conceptual and philosophical point of view. It lies in learning to think about not what architecture is, but what it can do: and doing it.
— Michael Fox

7. Cotton Grids in Berlin

In April 2004, on the podium of Mies van der Rohe's New National Gallery in Berlin, two small, colourful, airy structures were exposed to public view for a brief period of time. This spectacle in miniature was the launch of a new architectural product: Cotton Grid. Cotton Grid is a rectilinear space grid constructed of viscose embroidery thread, located and held taut in the pinpoints and incisions of a light, foamboard support. Cotton Grid evokes a curious perceptual effect, appearing to come to life before the eyes of the beholder, as if the coloured threads were dancing to a silent tune. This dancing sensation is complemented by moments of embodied atmosphere, as Cotton Grid appears to coalesce in the form of a bright, colourful cloud. Cotton Grid is thoroughly recommended for general enjoyment and moments of intense pleasure. The application of Cotton Grid to contemporary problems of building is currently in the early stages of development.
— Victoria Watson

8. The Funeral Parlour – A Contemporary Funeral Parlour for Client O'Rourke in London W12

The budget is £310,000 and completion was scheduled for June 2004. The black exterior marble surfaces of the funeral parlour will be inlaid with 2,000 chrome flower holders allowing the entire building to be covered in flowers. The parlour is divided into two zones: the open zone at the front acts as a continuation of the street and forms a portico-like space where people can gather and converse prior to entering the Chapel; and to the rear a private praying area allows a more intimate space directly surrounding the location of the coffin.
— Tom Teatum

9. 'Aut visum aut non' – Latin: You either see it or you don't

The work has no name – we cannot (and do not want to) find a definition to suit us. It hovers somewhere at the crossings of photography, architecture, spatial theory and travel writing. It is not developed along the established lines of any profession, but bits are borrowed from each of them. The photographs are captured without looking through the viewfinder, taken with a sense of touch rather than a sense of vision. They are about the world as much as pieces of it. Every picture is a relic of an event, a moment in a life that continues parallel to our own – parts in a developing story.
— noodleJam

10. The Right to Be Wrong ... 'Gonna Make a Mistake, Gonna Do it on Purpose' — Fiona Apple

The project: an electronic calculator that makes mistakes. Maybe it has happened already. Can you be really sure that your humble calculator is entirely faithful in its operation? Our trust in such technologies is so complete that, even when faced with a clearly incorrect answer, we would almost certainly put it down to an error on our own part. We might repeat the calculation and, this time, of course, it would be correct. It is the subtlety of the imperfection that is essential to the project.

A calculator that was merely defective would betray itself through degenerate behaviour. It might give an identical answer to every sum or refuse to display an answer at all. My mischievous calculator, on the other hand, will be entirely unpredictable in its failings. It might be a paragon of arithmetical perfection for years on end, before one day perversely declaring that 3x7 = 23. And when challenged to repeat its mistake, it will blithely revert to its former dependability. My calculators will find their way into banks, bars and brothels, faithfully executing mundane sums – most of the time. Slowly, however, doubts will begin to take hold. Rumours will begin to circulate of a fundamental unreliability in arithmetic. Henceforth, every simple sum will be open to dispute.

There is only one material reality, and consequently no alternative system of rules to take over when things fall apart. It is for this reason that the failure of a computer system is profoundly different from the failure of a biological organism. Though we might suffer injury, sickness or death, there is no discontinuity in the underlying organic processes. Matter and energy are in a constant state of flux. In contrast to artificial information-processing systems, the natural world is not based on anything.

Our world is increasingly ruled by arithmetic. In industrial societies, there are few areas of economic and cultural activity that remain untouched by information technology. Without wholly realising it we have surrendered to the seduction of the machine. In his book, *The Cyberiad*, Stanislaw Lem tells the story of an inventor who constructs an intelligent machine which, when asked the ritual question: How much is two plus two, gives the defiant answer – seven. Repeated adjustments and tinkering with the mechanism do nothing to improve matters. Though the inventor is disappointed, his friend is not entirely unimpressed – declaring:

There is no question but that we have here a stupid machine, and not merely stupid in the usual, normal way, oh no! This is ... the stupidest thinking machine in the entire world, and that's nothing to sneeze at! To construct deliberately, such a machine would be far from easy; in fact I would say that no one could manage it. For the thing is not only stupid, but stubborn as a mule.
— David Wilson

11. Sento (public bath)

Sento, the universal mark for public bath. Sento has been closely associated with city life for over 300 years in Japan, and is still a communal place for Japanese people of every generation. There are as many as 7,000 of these public baths throughout the country, of which approximately 1,300 are in central Tokyo. This one is located just off the Ginza main street, home of Bvlgari, Louis Vuitton, Prada *et al*. In a steamy hot bath, a 20-year-old would-be-designer, a corporate clean-shaven and an 80-year-old local resident celebrate a brief encounter, washing down their stress and sadness, sharing the moment, Gokuraku time.
— Miki Inamura

12. All the Way From America

Reading, Berkshire, commuter town and business park, is perhaps a fitting site for an experiment in democratic social engineering and architecture that rivals Archigram's smaller projects. In 1958, a peripatetic American speculator came to England with the notion of setting up some diners on the highways following US practice. Meanwhile, steaming across the Atlantic on a freighter were six ready-made diners from the Valentine Manufacturing Company of Wichita, Kansas. Discovering that the British planning authorities did not favour setting a diner down wherever there was a good passing trade, a deal had to be brokered with a catering-hotel-canteen chain who saw a chance to break the greasy-spoon transport café monopoly and feed the new motoring middle classes. On a backlot in the city centre, the first fully finished, air-conditioned Little Chef opened its sleek stainless-steel door. The others were planted at various far-flung sites about the Home Counties and Yorkshire moors. Such was the success of the 11 stool eateries that six more were ordered, and the operators set about copying the original design as a home-grown product. The original model had been drafted by an industrial designer schooled in aviation construction; the Reading version was made by producers of deep-fat fryers. It did not take off. After a general economic slump at the end of the 1960s, Little Chefs were farmed out to a timber-shed producer, and then made by local builders with the generic brief of providing a 40-seat restaurant that kept out the weather. There were 100 by 1972, and almost 300 by 1992, each effecting some semblance of agricultural, bungaloid, roses-round-the-door vernacular. Their banal mystery has even been compared to the melancholy spaces of Edward Hopper. Of the real steel diners, none remain; outgrown and outmoded visions of roadside culinary culture.

— David Lawrence

13. Visual Thinking

Visual thinking is a much more general phenomenon than occurs standing in front of a painting. Consider the following: the technology of film is based on a process in the eye called retinal blending. At a threshold of 24 frames per second, the human eye blends together a series of still images into a continuous flow. If the eye blends at a threshold of 24 frames, then flipping that fact, the eye can process 20 separate still frames each second. That means the average person, minus sleeping and blinking, has the capacity to take in a million images each day.

seeing→visualization→imagination→innovation→drawing→creativity

Writing down everything one sees in five minutes is an exhausting task. How many vivid images does one remember from a year? Seeing is not just the passive static of the mind taking in images like a sweater absorbing raindrops. It is the mental processing of the built environment, the cognition that goes into seeing a crumpled piece of paper on the ground and realising it is a five-pound note. It is visual awareness of surroundings – the ability to recognise a friend approaching on a train platform. It is the memory of shoe shopping with a friend who hates her toes, and thinks they look like little fingers.

If sight is taking in information from the outside world, mental visualisation is the idea of seeing inside one's head. It is what helps people win races or conquer stagefright – picturing ahead of time crossing the finish line or visualising 'the audience in their underwear'. My grandfather can go to the grocer's shop from memory, though his eyes fail him, as long as 'you tell me if there are any of those cardboard displays in the aisles'.

If visualisation is seeing inside one's head, imagination is creating those images. As Elliot Eisner, Stanford professor of art education, said: 'The central term in the word imagination is image. To imagine is to create new images that function in the creation of a new science, a new symphony, and in the design of a new bridge.'[1] The human mind rarely imagines purely in words, rather as that word suggests, in images. A visual awareness is required not just for visualising but for generating wholly new ideas. This is everything from wishful thinking to crisis aversion; from Bridget Jones receiving an email from Daniel Cleaver and instantly picturing them at their own wedding, to planning cars not to backfire, blow up or go over cliffs.

Imagination is also related to the question of how people understand each other. The Scottish philosopher Adam Smith's book *The Theory of Moral Sentiment* lays out an entire theory for understanding and judging the behaviour of other people solely through imagination. As Smith says (and he wrote in the 1700s, so substitute as one wishes for 'man'):

As we have no immediate experience of what other men feel, we can form no idea of the manner in which they are affected, but by conceiving what we ourselves should feel in the like situation. Though our brother is upon the rack, as long as we ourselves are at our ease, our senses will never inform us of what he suffers. They never did, and never can, carry us beyond our own person, and it is by the imagination only that we can form any conception of what are his sensations.[2]

Smith wrote convincingly that it is through imaginative exchanges that people understand, and misunderstand, each other. For instance, it is hard to sympathise with someone's emotional response if it is alienatingly strong. It is easier to relate to someone who appears to feel a bit down than to someone racked with unfathomable grief.

If taking in sensory information to makes one's own mental snapshots and paintings and films is an integrative sort of creativity, watching preordained sequences – part of the larger visual culture of media – is often passive, or at the least reactive. By constructed images, one could mean photographs or television or film, where a person or a group of people have carefully planned a whole image to see. It is not a matter of what would make a nice painting, it is being shown the painting itself. It is not watching a party, but being shown a film of one – seeing something through someone else's eyes or, often, as in the case of an advertisement, someone else's hopes and plans for how one will see it through one's own eyes. These questions are

"When man wanted to imitate walking he created the wheel, which does not resemble a leg. In the same way, he has created surrealism"
Apollinaire

▲▲▲▲ **Castors** 49mm. Max load 15kg
143.689.80 **£2/4pk**

not theoretical, but high-volume, multi-trillion-dollar businesses. In the US, 99 per cent of households have at least one television that stays on an average of 6 hours and 47 minutes each day. That means that the average adult is predicted to watch 70 days' worth of TV each year, and children spend 900 hours in school, but 1,500 hours in front of the TV. Altogether, Americans watch 250 billion hours of television in a year, which, billed at minimum wage, is $1.25 trillion (3 per cent of the US, approaching 1 per cent of the world economy).[3]

As to the American school-age children who spend 1,680 minutes in front of the television each week, in contrast they spend 3.5 minutes in meaningful conversation with their parents. And, if given the option of spending time with their fathers or watching TV, 54 per cent are likely to go for the television instead. By the time these same children finish elementary school, they will have seen 8,000 murders or violent acts on television. By their 18th birthdays, that number has leapt to 200,000. 59 per cent of Americans can name the Three Stooges – compared to 17 per cent who can name at least three of the Supreme Court justices. Advertisers capitalise on this fact by spending $15 billion on TV ads each year.

In the hours outside of watching television, one can always catch a film. Globally, there are 99,000 cinemas, which attract 6.7 billion visitors each year. People go to see one of roughly 2,300 feature films distributed each year.[4] And if one misses a film, there is also video rental: 6 million rentals, which compares to 3 million library books, checked out each year in the US. Seeing is an industry as well as a basic skill.

**— Edited excerpt from 'Museum Legs/Art School',
an unpublished book by Amy Whitaker, written whilst
attending the postgraduate fine art course at the
Slade School of Art, UCL, London 2003–04.**

Notes
1 Elliot Eisner, *The Kind of Schools We Need*, p 25.
2 1,1, Para 2, p 9.
3 The 70 hours figure comes from the US census: www.census.gov/Press-Release/www/releases/archives/facts_for_features_speci... 30/04/2004. CB04-FFSE.04. All other figures on TV come from: 'The Sourcebook for Teaching Science': www.csun.edu/~vceed002/health/docs/tv&health.html (30 April 2004).
5 UNESCO stats: www.uis.unesco.org/ev.php.

14. **Being On Wheels**

a. This cargo wagon, which also carried horses, was manufactured from wood and metal in Hungary in the 1950s. Originally owned by the Organisation of the Greek Railway of Greece, it travelled to and from eastern and central Europe. It is now in northern Greece, close to Nea Iraklia, 40 kilometres south of Thessaloniki, on the coast. Being on wheels, it requires no planning permission. Not involving excessive expense or bureaucracy, it is a popular solution for summer houses. Add roofs and terraces, take two wagons and join them together or insulate to provide a year-round home. Grow trees for shade. Another method that avoids planning permission is to carry out construction work during the night.

b. Pay and Display Parking. PAY AND DISPLAY USERS: PARK ONLY IN PAY AND DISPLAY BAYS. NO CHANGE GIVEN. Pay to park, display what you've paid. Display ticket inside front windscreen. A PENALTY NOTICE WILL BE ISSUED FOR FAILURE TO DISPLAY A VALID TICKET IN A MARKED BAY OR FOR NOT PARKING WHOLLY WITHIN THE PAY AND DISPLAY BAY.
{Backlit Projection on Front Windscreen.}

c. Wheel Envy. A couple make love. Afterwards, the woman is laid out, relaxed and satiated. She rolls her head to the side and catches sight of a cartwheel, and is suddenly jealous of the wheel for always having its axle. (Part-remembered story from an anonymous Sanskrit love poem.)

d. Castors. A Moment, when time is for any whim of the mind, where everything and nothing can collide. I am flicking through an Ikea catalogue absorbed into the potential that my home both has and hasn't got. Then, page 291, Ikea Storage: Keep Everything in Perspective, the Antonius range, item #7, Castors. The Castor, attached to an object, holding the potential for the static to become mobile, younger sibling of the wheel, with its binding relationship to revolutions. Is the lowly Castor not one of our most important yet least realised ideals?
— bceeg ⌂

Art historian **Marie-Ange Brayer** is director of the Centre Regional Contemporary Art Collection (FRAC Centre) in Orléans, France, the collection of which focuses on the relation between art and architecture. The FRAC Centre is developing a collection of architecture in its experimental dimension, from the 1960s to the present day. Brayer has organised many exhibitions of this collection, both in France and abroad (London, Beijing, Budapest, Siena, New York and Tokyo). As cofounder of ArchiLab, the international architectural conference held in Orléans, which since 1999 has annually brought together a new, forward-looking generation of architects, she is also preparing a PhD at the School of Advanced Studies in Social Sciences (EHESS) in Paris on the architectural maquette from the Renaissance onwards.

Nic Clear is a registered architect who teaches at the Bartlett School of Architecture where he runs Unit 15, a postgraduate design unit that specialises in the use of video, animation and motion graphics. A founding director of the now defunct General Lighting and Power, he now divides his time between writing fiction and making drawings and films. He has exhibited his work internationally, and has curated a number of shows, including 'People Objects Movement Time – New Video Animation in Architecture' in January 2005. He is also the lead singer of the industrial country and western covers band Fat Midget.

Liza Fior is a founding partner of muf architecture/art, which was established in 1994 with the then eccentric ambition of working exclusively in the public realm. The firm continues to do so. Current projects include: a landscaped route over a 6-metre-high sewer embankment that in turn creates an informal amphitheatre to a previously isolated park in East London; a museum pavilion to house a Roman mosaic, constructed from GRC panels of crushed oyster shell; a choreographed boat journey along a derelict stretch of canal on the brink of redevelopment for an invited audience of residents, developers, regeneration officers, social activists and trades unionists; and underpasses, alleyways and large tracts of undesignated land – an urban audit with design proposals of open spaces that are not parks in East London.

Jon Goodbun is a lecturer in architectural history and theory at the University of Westminster, and a partner in the practice WaG Architecture. He is a previous winner of the RIBA Silver Medal Tutor Prize and has published previously on Tafuri, Modernism and Las Vegas. **David Cunningham** is a lecturer in literature and critical theory at the University of Westminster, and an editor of the journal *Radical Philosophy*. He has published on surrealism, as well as on the avant-garde, Beckett, Adorno and architectural theory, amongst other topics. Together, Goodbun and Cunningham have guest-edited (with Karin Jaschke) a special issue of *The Journal of Architecture* on postwar avant-garde movements, and are currently coediting (with David Lomas) a book on surrealism and architecture. Both are members of the Polytechnic Research Group at Westminster.

Professor John Hamilton Frazer is international research co-coordinator for the Gehry Technologies Digital Project Ecosystem. He has been pioneering the development of intelligent and interactive building design systems and evolutionary design computation for more than 30 years. His research in this field has been developed at the AA in London, Cambridge University, the University of Ulster, and at the Hong Kong Polytechnic University where he was Swire Chair Professor, head of the School of Design and director of the Design Technology Research Centre. He is the founder of Autotectonica and was chairman of the award-winning Autographics software development company. His seminal book, *An Evolutionary Architecture* (AA, 1995) is now available to download free through the AA website: www.aaschool.ac.uk/publications/ea/intro.html.

Samantha Hardingham trained at the Architectural Association (1987–93). She is the author of a number of books including the first in the highly acclaimed ellipsis guide book series, *London: A Guide to Recent Architecture* (now published by Batsford/Chrysalis), and *Cedric Price Opera* (Wiley-Academy, 2003). She is currently a research fellow at the Research Centre for Experimental Practice (EXP) based in the Department of Architecture at the University of Westminster.

Timothy Jachna received his Bachelor of Architecture degree from the University of Illinois at Chicago, and a diploma from the Architectural Association. He has worked as an architect and urban designer in Chicago, Athens and Berlin. He is currently teaching and researching at the School of Design of the Hong Kong Polytechnic University and pursuing a PhD on digital urbanism in China with the Spatial Information Architecture Lab at RMIT in Melbourne.

Nicholas Lister studied architecture at the University of Westminster where he founded Flying Circus, the student architectural society, and led the group to some notoriety through several projects. He has been elected to a seat on the RIBA Council and is now involved in education as a member of the ARCHAOS executive team. Past work on a number of architectural projects includes Primary Space. He currently works for ESA.

James Madge studied architecture at Cambridge University. After working in the offices of David Roberts (Cambridge) and Camberwell Borough Architect, he combined private practice with teaching (Architectural Association, Thames Polytechnic, PCL/University of Westminster) with the emphasis progressively shifting from the former to the latter. He has written on a variety of topics in a number of architectural publications.

Will McLean trained at the Architectural Association (1987–93). He is co-head of technical studies, with Pete Silver, at the University of Westminster. Together they are co-authoring a book on fabrication processes in the UK. McLean is currently working on a number of design projects with artist Bruce McLean, including a primary school in North Ayrshire and an interactive light sculpture for Blackpool promenade. He is soon to author a forthcoming regular feature of $\triangle$+.

Christopher Moller was born in New Zealand. He studied industrial design before qualifying in architecture in 1984 at Auckland University. He gained experience on urban and architectural projects in New Zealand, and at the same time was secretary for the Wellington Architecture Centre, involved in saving buildings and changing attitudes to urban policy. He later worked in Hong Kong and the UK before cofounding S333 Architecture + Urbanism in 1990. He worked as a senior urbanist for the City of Groningen in the Netherlands, and is a member of the GRAS architecture centre Think Tank. He teaches at the Academy of Architecture in Groningen, and was design tutor at the Post Graduate Housing and Urbanism Unit at the Architectural Association from 1995 to 2001.

Jon Vincent is a garden designer. His company, Flora Gardens, operates from West London and has won awards for excellence and many prestigious contracts throughout its 12-year history. A unique style has evolved through diverse influences such as gardens by Roberto Burle Marx, photographs by Martin Parr, supermarket car parks and motorway verges. Examples of his work can be seen at www.floragardens.co.uk.

Robert Webb is an architect and engineer specialising in sustainable energy design solutions. He leads the studio XCO2 in providing energy engineering and design for low-carbon solutions in the built environment. XCO2 works in partnership with architects, developers and housing providers to optimise environmental performance within elegant designs and at no additional cost.

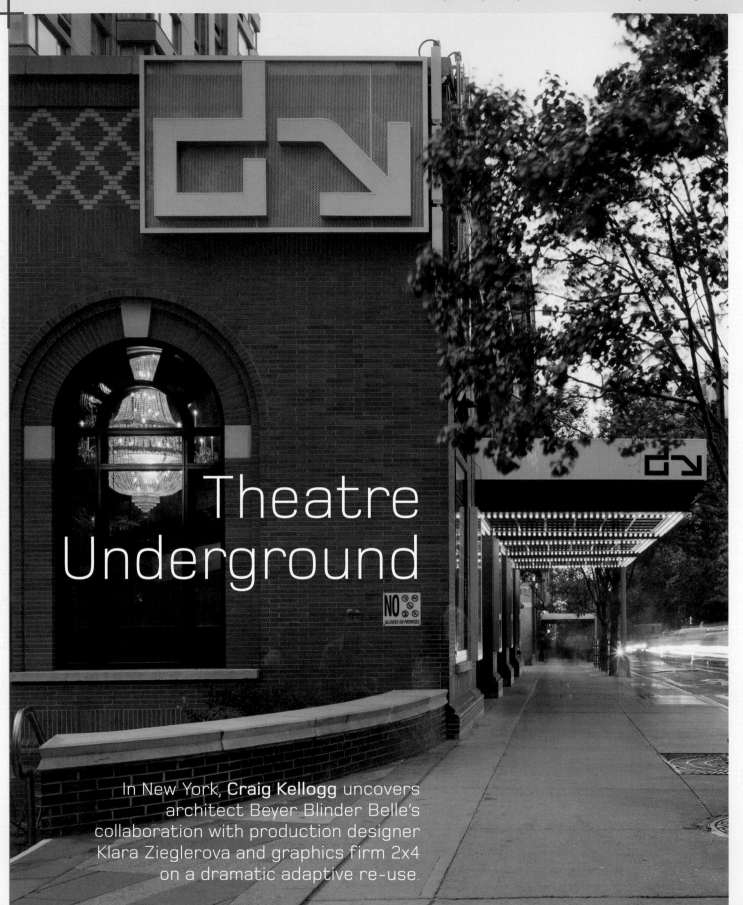

Beyer Blinder Belle, Klara Zieglerova and 2x4, Dodger Stages theatres,
New York City, 2004
Below
In Midtown Manhattan, an outsize new chandelier and blunt modern signage offer clues about the conversion of underground cinemas into a theatrical multiplex with space for up to five live performances running simultaneously.

Theatre Underground

In New York, **Craig Kellogg** uncovers architect Beyer Blinder Belle's collaboration with production designer Klara Zieglerova and graphics firm 2x4 on a dramatic adaptive re-use.

Off-off-Broadway productions play in cramped black-painted rooms or worse, to audiences often seated in mismatched chairs. A lucky few shows eventually swap this squalor for larger rooms, en route to the big Broadway houses. Midtown Manhattan once boasted plenty of the necessary medium-sized venues, built originally for legitimate theatre or vaudeville and the other burlesques. But decades ago, in the name of modernisation, history saw the majority fitted with permanent cinema screens, if not chopped into multiplex cinemas with sticky floors and a popcorn concession.

Today cinemas are as common in New York as venues for live theatre once were, and the majority of multiplexes are purpose-built to occupy places considered unpromising for other uses. So it was with the 1989 Worldwide Cinemas, shoehorned into a basement between two Manhattan high-rises in a mixed-use redevelopment. The subterranean facility lies directly beneath a small, underused outdoor plaza with curving paths and a fountain at the centre. 'The very depressing character of the basement did not help,' says Dick Blinder, a founding partner of Beyer Blinder Belle Architects & Planners.

Business was slow, and Worldwide Cinemas had begun selling cut-price tickets to hopelessly stale movies when the regularly scheduled screenings ended abruptly several years ago. For Beyer Blinder Belle, which specialises in preservation, the site represented a chance to reverse the historical trend. The theatrical producer Dodger Stage Holding ultimately invested US$20 million in converting the 5,700-square-metre cinemas for – ironically – live performances, adding a small bar accessible to the public, and new mezzanines reached via bridges. A completely reconfigured double-height underground central lobby is set against new panels of backlit metal mesh.

Now, nearly 2,000 patrons at a time can attend five live productions running simultaneously in converted cinemas that range in size from 200 to 500 seats. Several months after the opening, the decidedly offbeat tenants included 'Symphonie Fantastique', an hour-long rhapsody performed by puppeteers hovering above a 1,000-gallon tank of illuminated water, and the scantily clad 'Pieces (of Ass)', which deals with 'themes uniquely common to the physically blessed female'. On a more informal basis, the central underground lobby for all the theatres can be furnished as a café-style venue for late-night stand-up comedy performances.

The Dodgers charged the independent Czech-born theatrical designer Klara Zieglerova with styling the public interiors. Zieglerova, who has created productions for both stage (the musical 'Saturday Night Fever') and screen ('You've Got Mail') had visited the space in its previous incarnation. 'Everybody knew it as the cheap theatre,' she says, neatly summing up her challenge. The subterranean interiors were all spongy acoustic ceilings and loud broadloom wall-to-wall. 'I asked them to demolish everything that was not structural,' she adds.

The transformation becomes evident along West 50th Street, where the original pavement-level entry pavilion sports blunt new signage by the graphics firm 2x4. Mouldings and

bric-a-brac were banished inside the once-Postmodern lobby in favour of smooth silvery walls. And Zieglerova supplied her own instantly recognisable icon, in the form of an outsized 3-metre-tall chandelier visible from the street through the Palladian window. The main stairway descends beneath the chandelier towards the concessions and individual theatres below ground.

Belle explains that the team was charged with 'creating impact at the lowest possible cost', in part because of expensive back-of-house and structural modifications. Yellow supergraphics by 2x4 are painted directly on the exposed concrete floor, like the markings on an airfield. Fluorescent tubes stream laser-like overhead, below the ceiling's exposed guts and mechanicals. (Zieglerova has picked them out with moody coloured illumination.) Hard-edged and coolly futuristic, the overall effect is crisp, like the digital world conjured in the 1982 film *Tron*, in this case as interpreted by a Philippe Starck type. In fact, some of the surreal focal furnishings scattered around are straight from the Dodgers' prop warehouse, for example a gold-leafed settee and the lime dressmakers' dummies.

Zieglerova used the same shocking green to highlight the deeply corrugated structure underneath the main stairway, which was exposed during construction. Other demolition

allowed Beyer Blinder Belle to reconfigure the mezzanine bridges for public access to the new balconies added in the theatres. Stadium-style seating on risers replaced the formerly flat theatre floors.' By today's standards of stadium seating, they were old-fashioned,' Belle notes. Otherwise, the venues themselves are essentially neutral black boxes without prosceniums. Sightlines and theatrical infrastructure were overseen by theatre consultant Sach Morgan Studio, providing a base for gadgets that tenants will add as needed. 'Very often if you provide those things, the production company wants to do something else anyway,' Blinder says.

New soundproofing throughout helps to quieten the footfalls of people clicking across the plaza overhead. To limit migration of stray noises through the air ducts, new individual mechanical systems offer each venue acoustic isolation. The architects also beefed up the walls between theatres, correcting a problem common in multiplex cinemas. With live theatre, you can't just turn up the volume to mask any distractions. Despite the references to *Tron*, performances at Dodger Stages are most certainly not a cyborg fantasy overlaid with a booming soundtrack. At least not yet. ⚙+

Below
Royal Dutch Embassy, Ljubljana, 2002
Bevk and Perovic designed this residence
for both public and private space.

Bevk Perovic arhitekti

An exciting new crop of young Slovenian architects is coming out of Ljubljana. **Valentina Croci** explores the work of Bevk Perovic arhitekti, a practice whose finely honed hybrid approach owes as much to the contextualism of the great Ljubljanan master Joze Plecnik, as Vasa Perovic's exposure to contemporary Dutch architectural thought and design at the Berlage Institute in Amsterdam.

The faceless outskirts of Ljubljana are distinguished by newly built commercial office blocks and apartment blocks of a dubious quality. This is, though, merely the superficial aspect of a city the historic core of which is the stage set for the planning and architectural schemes of one of the greatest modern masters – Joze Plecnik. As the capital city of the now independent Republic of Slovenia, Ljubljana faces the challenge of reconciling the speculative demands of an economic system based on free enterprise with the cultural traditions and political and social situation of a country until recently under communist rule.

Still recovering from the aftermath of war, Slovenia is now a fully fledged member of the ever-expanding European Union, and in the last decade Ljubljana has grown significantly, in part to meet the demands of the

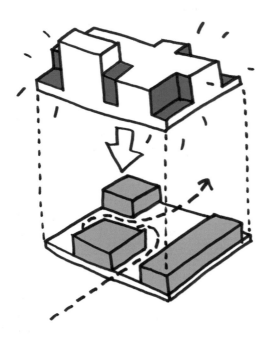

influx of refugees or evacuees from the former Yugoslavia. A kind of 'silent' architecture designed by a new generation of Slovenian architects has made its appearance in the city: seemingly non-astonishing, it nonetheless contains carefully planned and updated elements of vernacular building traditions. Both positive and negative architectural models define this 'vernacular' character. On the one hand are the traditional detached houses in Gorenjska, the region to the north of Ljubljana, which are characterised by their wooden cladding, or the efficient 1950s and 1960s apartment blocks in the centre of the city. However, on the other hand, at the periphery of Ljubljana the vernacular is defined by a sort of low-profile housing that has arisen over the last 50 years – banal two-storey detached houses, mainly in concrete, at the centre of small green plots.

This new generation of architects has its epicentre in Ljubljana – Bevk Perovic, Dekleva-Gregoric, Elastic, Maechtig-Vrhunc, Ofis, Sadar-Vuga, to cite just a few. All are in their 30s, and were studying abroad during the period of passage from socialist regime to capitalist democracy, and having found its own area of design investigation in the hybridisation of Western architectural theories and models applied to the local political and cultural context, this new generation is now rapidly gaining attention in international cultural circles.[1] Though they experienced a world in which architecture is practised as a global phenomenon, with a star system that encourages the development of self-important and narcissistic styles, their work reveals a strong attachment to place. These young firms are developing a personal set of preoccupations, closely related to the inherent situation in Slovenia. Each has achieved a coherent expressive language, and a stable and well-resolved architecture, yet remains permeable to a variety of influences. Thus, architecture becomes a subversive terrain. It contains both poetics and the capacity to contemplate change.

Among these architects, Vasa Perovic and Matija Bevk are key to an understanding of the process of the hybridisation of Western models and ties to local culture. Dealing mainly with non-profit or low-cost apartment blocks, Bevk Perovic arhitekti did not harden into obvious formal citations of the local architectural language or traditional housing types, as in the redefinition of these types in response to legislative variables and local planning regulations.

Vasa Perovic was born in Belgrade, graduated from the city's faculty of architecture, and completed a masters in design with Herman Hertzberger in 1994 at the Berlage Institute of Architecture in Amsterdam. He moved to Slovenia to oversee his project for the Kocevje Primary School, a competition he won in 1995. And it was this experience that led to his desire to remain in the country in order to confront some of the challenges posed by the local situation with sensitivity and a fresh outlook. In 1997, with Slovenian partner Matija Bevk, he founded Bevk Perovic arhitekti in Ljubljana.

Bevk is a graduate of the faculty of architecture of the University of Ljubljana. Like Perovic, he has travelled widely in Europe, especially in Holland. 'I developed my architectural personality while studying at the Berlage,' explains Perovic. 'At the time, architectural composition was taught based on a leftist political agenda.' In fact, traces of the theories of Elia Zengelis and Kenneth Frampton (tutors of Perovic's thesis), and of Herman Hertzberger, dean of the Berlage at the time, appear throughout the work of Bevk Perovic arhitekti: the social function of the building, the clarity of the building programme, and the idea that the

Top, middle and bottom
B S/B private house, Ljubljana, 2002
Even though this residential house is wide open to the street with its large front window, the privacy of the owners is well preserved from the outside as the layout, over two floors, is such that the spaces where all daily activities take place are oriented towards the backyard. A system of sliding doors makes the interior spaces highly flexible.

building's identity is determined by the lives within. Other characteristics are the use of basic low-cost materials that permit part of the budget to be devoted to the creation of exterior public spaces, considered an integral part of the project. References to Dutch architecture can thus be found in this rational and social approach to design.

The work of Bevk Perovic is quite different from that of a studio such as MVRDV. The latter seek to reinvent reality through the violation of the rules of architectural schools and established building types, and their projects always contain an underlying utopian character. Bevk Perovic is also distant from the visionary and philosophical approach of such architectural stars as Rem Koolhaas, who have transferred the themes of architectural design and planning problems to a speculative and global level. The firm always conducts its design investigations on a local scale. While its work reveals an obvious familiarity with Dutch architecture, Bevk and Perovic clarify that it is only a matter of outward appearances. A quest for 'unusual' forms is not the aim of their work. According to Perovic: 'Every decision regarding form represents a solution to an objective problem. For example, because of cost and time constraints, the structural detailing at the windows of the Zeleni Gaj apartment complex is repeated across every facade, characterising the appearance of the building.'

The opening up of contemporary Slovenian architecture towards Western models is helping to relieve Slovenia from its geographical and cultural isolation, and involving its architects

in international architectural debates. However, there is a danger of an uncritical, a priori adoption of Western models. 'A risk common to all new members of the European Union – that is the economically weaker border countries – is the indiscriminate cancellation of cultural distinctiveness in favour of dominant models,' claim Bevk and Perovic.

The architects cite the local architectural heritage, high in quality and developed in part through the teachings of Joze Plecnik and his students Edo Ravnikar, Savin Sever and Stanko Kristl at the school of architecture of Ljubljana in the 1950s and 1960s. Plecnik, a student of Otto Wagner and active in Ljubljana from 1921 to 1957, in particular embodies the Slovenian spirit and architectural tradition. Going beyond stylistic trends, he developed his poetics through a deep knowledge of materials and the study of a compositional syntax that precludes a dogmatic use of building typologies. The language of Plecnik is quite distant from the outcomes of Modernism. Nonetheless, his architecture is just as innovative, both for its capacity to create new codes from traditional architectural forms, both classical and vernacular, and for its inventive approach to plan. An example is the St Francis of Assisi church (1925–30) in the Siska quarter of Ljubljana. Quadrangular in plan and without naves, the interior space is surrounded by a peristyle.

Based on the architecture of Plecnik, Bevk and Perovic have developed their own approach to 'contextualism': the building must relate to the surrounding buildings and landscape, establishing its place in the urban hierarchy. For example, in designing the B S/B private house in Ljubljana, the architects began with a volume based on the typical two-storey buildings that constellate the capital city's streets. The two levels were separated to form an L-shape that defines two sides of a garden looking onto the woods. A window on the upper floor runs the length of the main facade along the street. Allowing light to enter without disturbing the privacy of the inhabitants, the window is the main compositional element of the facade. In a similar approach, the architects clad the upper floor of their building for the Dutch Embassy in Ljubljana (2002) with strips of light-coloured wood,

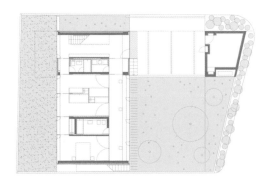

emphasising the private nature of this top floor, and citing the use of wood in the houses of Gorenjska. The firm's attention to detail is not decorative in purpose. Rather, it is an attempt to transfer the local cultural heritage to a contemporary and more general model.

Non-Profit Housing Types

Bevk Perovic arhitekti has designed several non-profit apartment complexes. Since the foundation of the Republic of Slovenia in 1991, and the ensuing wars of succession, there has been an urgent need to offer asylum to refugee populations and political refugees from the former Yugoslavia, though the need for apartments in the cities had already become urgent during the last years of the socialist government. 'This emergency situation has caused a loss of the high quality and attention to detail that have characterised the local architectural tradition, a typical example of which are the apartment complexes designed by Savin Sever and Stanko Kristl in the 1950s and 1960s,' explains Perovic. During the 1990s, in fact, many developers took advantage of government incentives, building a large number of extremely low-quality housing blocks. Speculation in the property market on the part of the private sector is quite risky. The government is now attempting to remedy the problem by aiding low-income families through low-interest home loans and a programme of non-profit housing managed by the individual municipalities. But, unfortunately, this has failed to reduce the construction of ugly, substandard building complexes.

'We are one of the very few architectural firms in Slovenia that specifically designs social housing without treating it as a speculative and financial operation. We consider our quest for low-cost solutions that afford a high quality of life as an interesting architectural and political opportunity.' The projects presented here posed some extremely difficult problems: low budgets, high density on small plots, restrictive building and planning laws, and often unpleasant surroundings. However, the architects have transformed these limitations into the driving forces of their design process.

In designing a complex in the Polje quarter of Ljubljana, the architects began with the relationship between the landscape and the building plot, bordered to one side by railway tracks. They placed the car park and a green area next to the tracks in order to reduce the impact of noise and to distance the buildings from the railway. The communal gardens and play areas were organised along the longitudinal axis of the site. It was not easy to find room for these spaces because, given the height limits and the required number of floors, the remaining area would not have been sufficient to accommodate the 80 apartments. However, another restriction imposed upon the project – the sloped form of the roof – meant that the architects could maximise the volumes of these attic spaces by varying the roof slopes, thus creating additional living areas wherever the heights were sufficient for habitation. The unusual roof slopes became an aesthetic feature of the project, together with the facade patterns, which reflect variations on

the interior. In fact, the layouts were differentiated, based on a variety of models, to avoid the standardisation typical of low-cost rental housing.

Bevk Perovic arhitekti emphasises the importance of a well-designed plan. For example, in the non-profit housing complex in the city of Maribor (ongoing), the architects mitigated the problem of the small size of the apartments and lack of amenities in the communal areas by creating double-height glazed spaces within the volume of the building. 'This superimposing of public and private spaces might appear to be a citation of Dutch architecture – for example, projects by Kees Christiaanse in the early 1990s,' explains Perovic, 'however, this particular solution derives from the resolution of a specific problem, that is the need to create social spaces in a volume that is too small for the prescribed number of inhabitants.' Not even the architects can predict whether the mix of public and private space in the Maribor apartments will work: analogous projects in the 1970s were not successful. Nonetheless, they represent an attempt to render life less alienating.

Among the architects' latest social housing projects is an apartment complex for political refugees. The programme for this project was even more complex because the building is a primary shelter for refugees, who are only supposed to reside there for a limited time. The architects thus found themselves dealing with such concepts as 'home', 'alienation' and cultural 'belonging', all of which are represented by precise architectural decisions. Furthermore, the low-cost building plots are generally located far from transport and other services, at the risk of further alienating the refugee population. ⌂+

Social Housing Complex, Polje, Ljubljana, 2002–04
The Polje complex was built on a site bordered by a busy road and railway tracks. The architects located the car park and the green areas near the tracks, and the communal spaces between the buildings. To avoid noise problems, the buildings do not face onto the play areas. The facades reflect the variation of the various floors. In fact, while each floor contains four apartments, there is a certain degree of flexibility both in the layout of the apartments, based on several schemes, and in the internal divisions, left to the discretion of the owner. The non-standardisation of the various floors is reflected by the fact that the balconies and windows are not vertically aligned. Insulating cement-fibre cladding panels, attached by means of projecting spikes, generate an interesting pattern, which, together with the rust colour of the panels, allude to the nearby railway.

Box Projects
Zeleni Gaj apartments, Siska area, Ljubljana, 1999–2001

The Zeleni Gaj district of Ljubljana was the first experience of non-profit housing for the Bevk Perovic arhitekti. Designed to host the elderly, the complex was then placed on the property market. Repetition throughout of the structural detailing of the windows lowered construction costs whilst increasing visual interest. The housing for the metal window frames was created within the structural elements in reinforced concrete, and the window units were later inserted from within, in a special 'sandwich' system. The exterior plaster was textured with coarse sand, resulting in a low-cost, light-reflecting surface. The balconies take the form of loggias inside the perimeter of the apartments, making it possible to vary the layout of the apartments without adding projecting structures that would have modified the structural characteristics of the building.

Social Housing Complex, Maribor, 2002–

In an attempt to mitigate the sense of alienation commonly experienced by the inhabitants of large apartment blocks, Bevk Perovic arhitekti provided places to socialise by inserting double-height glazed communal spaces within the buildings of the 130-apartment complex. The scheme resulted in pleasant spaces that receive abundant natural light and add variation to the composition of the elevations. The framed projecting loggias and the undulated metal cladding of the facades are examples of the Slovenian firm's original, low-cost solutions. Though the loggias, the metal cladding, and the horizontal strips in correspondence to the floors all act as decorative elements of the facade, they have mainly functional purposes. The site is adjacent to a busy road, and the building was therefore oriented to create safe children's play areas.

Valentina Croci is a freelance journalist. She has been part of the editorial staff of *Ottagono*, an Italian monthly on industrial design and architecture, for three years. She contributed to the first issue of the *OP* series of architectural monographs, on Santiago Calatrava. She graduated at the Venice Institute of Architecture (IUAV), achieved an MSc in architectural history from the Bartlett School of Architecture, and has recently been offered a place for the PhD in product and communication design at the IUAV.

[Translation by Maureen Young]

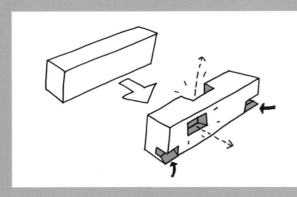

Note
1 '6IXPack: Contemporary Slovenian Architecture', catalogue of the exhibition, edited by Andrej Hrausky, produced by DESSA and 6IXPack architects, Vale-Novak publisher (Ljubljana), 2004. The Slovenian Ministry of Foreign Affairs is sponsoring the exhibition as a promotional event for Slovenia as a new member of the EU. It is also part of a wider programme for promoting the country through its culture and art. In fact, an exhibition about Plecnik will be featured, as well as two exhibitions of industrial and fashion design.

Resumé

Bevk Perovic arhitekti

1995
Vasa Perovic (with N Dodd, A Vehovar and T Glazar) wins competition for the Kocevje Primary School.

1997
Matija Bevk and Vasa Perovic found Bevk Perovic studio in Ljubljana.
First prize in competition for row houses in Koseze, Ljubljana (built 2000–02).

1998
First prize in competition for the housing quarter in Crnuce, Ljubljana.

1999
Zeleni Gaj apartments, Siska, Ljubljana (built 2000–01)
Study commission for the faculty of mathematics and physics, Ljubljana University.

2000
Housing settlement Jurckova pot 2 in Ljubljana: urban study commission.
Worker hostel in Ljubljana: study commission.
First prize in competition for the Cesca vas housing quarter, Novo Mesto.

2001
Non-profit housing in Dolgi Most, Ljubljana: study for the urban project.

2002
Social housing complex of 130 units in Maribor, in progress.
Social housing complex, Polje, Ljubljana, in progress.
Completion of B S/B private house, Ljubljana.
Completion of House Luks, Piran.
Housing complex of 25 units in Rijeka, Croatia, in progress.
Completion of Royal Dutch Embassy, Ljubljana.
Completion of Kocevje Primary School; receives Piranesi International Prize for Architecture
Plecnik Prize for Architecture for Zeleni Gaj apartments

2003
Refugee hotel, 130 units, Ljubljana, in progress.
Faculty of mathematics and physics, Ljubljana University, in progress.
'6IXPack: Contemporary Slovenian Architecture', ongoing exhibition and catalogue (edited in 2004).
Design for 'The Structure of Survival' exhibition curated by Carlos Basualdo, Venice Biennale of Art.

2004
Two social housing projects, Ljubljana: study commission.
130-unit housing development, Ljubljana ring road, in progress.
Headquarters for a stone-mining company, invited competition.
Technological park in Ljubljana, invited competition.
Apartment renovation, Zagreb, Croatia.
Interior design for Ljubljana advertising agency.

HLT, **Opera House, Copenhagen, 2001–04**
Top
The axial relationship across the waterway to the 19th-century church is a
crucial generator of the design, and part of its anchor to history and context.

Bottom
The Opera House sits on a former naval dockyard in the
Dokøen island in the north harbour district of Copenhagen.

Opera House
Copenhagen

Jeremy Melvin describes how Henning Larsen Tegnestue's design for the new Opera House in Copenhagen, on the site of an old naval dockyard, was driven as much by a desire to connect with the city as by the finest auditorium.

Top left
Copenhagen is reconfiguring itself by placing major public
institutions in new buildings on former dockland, but retaining the
working waterways. The building site in the distance will house the
new Royal Theatre. Audiences can arrive at the door of the Opera
House by boat, something that is not possible at any other opera
house, even at Venice's La Fenice.

Top right
The foyers have a crisp and elegant feel – and Olufur Eliasson's chandeliers.

Middle
Traditional in form but modern in feel, the auditorium is both intimate and grand.

Bottom
The subterranean orchestra rehearsal room simulates natural light.

'I want the best auditorium you can get': Maersk Mc-Kinney
Møller's instruction to Henning Larsen Tegnestue (HLT) for a
new opera house in Copenhagen could not have been more
direct and specific. As he was picking up the £250 million tab
from his personal fortune, he had every right to make his
wishes known. HLT's position and status as architects, though,
led the firm to two realisations. First, they did not have the
necessary expertise to deliver something so technically
sophisticated as the best possible auditorium; and second, as
architects they believed strongly that even the best auditorium
has to be grounded in its urban context. The design's success
would rest on achieving both aims, ensuring a degree of
continuity between experiencing opera under the finest
possible conditions and the relationship to its surroundings,
and indeed the possible readings of the city that audiences
might bring with them.

Addressing the first issue meant finding specialist advice,
however for the second HLT could draw deeply on its
knowledge of Copenhagen and experience of introducing large
new institutions into it. Since the early 1990s, many
constituent parts of the city have changed. With the dispersal
of the port, largely due to the opening of the Øresund crossing
to Malmö in Sweden, large tracts of waterfront land close to
the city centre have become derelict and, rather than letting
them fester, the authorities have commissioned master plans
and designated sites for large new institutions to act as focal
points on them. From a tight, inward-looking core ringed by
waterways, the city now looks outwards with a dialogue
emerging between large developments on either side of the
wide waterways.

HLT has itself experienced this change in a particular way.
In the early 1990s the firm designed a new building entirely

Top
The canteen for staff and performers

Bottom
On the upper levels, staggered bridges take the audience into the auditorium.

The clarity of exterior expression continues on the inside. Under the roof is a bulbous and largely glass foyer, its shape seeming to come from carrying the load of the roof and in response to the curves of the auditorium rather than a whim. It is a wonderful space, taking advantage of 180 degree views on several levels, its several tiers linked by staircases and leading into the auditorium across bridges at a different angle on each level.

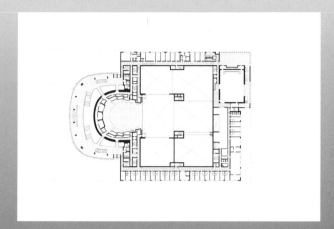

within the existing confines of the Ny Carlsberg Glyptotek museum, but since then has undertaken several projects on the old port frontage. As well as a major commercial and residential complex for a bank, it master-planned the north port area and designated the site where the Opera House now stands – once a naval dockyard – for a public institution. Old warehouses immediately behind have already become schools for architecture, film and other creative disciplines as well as the inevitable loft dwellings. Land on either side of the Opera House site was scheduled for 40,000 square metres of residential space, with retail and other service activities at ground level. Ever aware of the problems of dispersal, HLT even proposed a new car park under the water, with exits on either side of the channel – one to the old centre and the other to the new institutions.

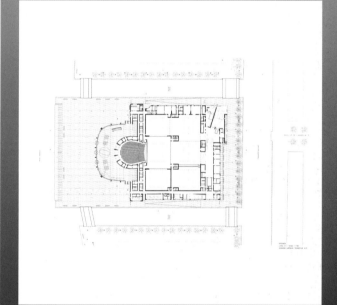

The architects' detailed reading of the location proved the key to balancing the Opera House's two priorities. Working with Arup Acoustics and Theatre Planning and Technology helped to meet Møller's ambitions for the auditorium, but the presence on the other side of the water of Marmorkirken – a domed, 19th-century neoclassical church – implied an axis that the Opera House could strengthen. The axis also passes through the Amelienborg Castle, and as such cements the symbolic connection between the city's historic and emerging districts and, in a piquant touch, reflects that both church and Opera House are the gifts of super-rich industrialists. The axis would naturally culminate in the auditorium; however, HLT was determined that the connection should be active rather than passive. Consequently, at stalls level there are giant doors echoing the entrance doors to the church, and if both sets open simultaneously, altar could face stage, with foyers, streets, a park and waterway in between. It is the sort of connection between city and stage that Schinkel sought in his famous set design in the Berlin Schauspielhaus, which projected the building's setting into the scenery.

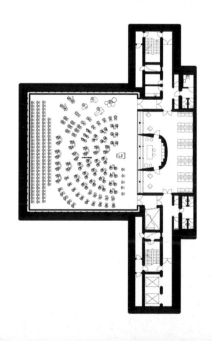

Despite the intervening layers of public and private space, the connection between the primary elements has a great clarity that must owe something to the simple and powerful forms. The huge oversailing roof both reinforces the directionality and creates a giant outdoor space in front of the Opera House. Boats might land here, or it could even be configured as an outdoor arena with performers on the water. It is a powerful gesture, but the intended buildings on either side would make more sense of it. However, the overall effect is to connect the spiritual – art and religion – through their messy interfaces with ordinary life yet without undue dilution. Architecture and urban design here shadow the primary purpose of opera, to transfigure experiences into universal archetypes through the most rarified of dramatic techniques. Richard Wagner and his architectural collaborator Gottfried Semper would certainly have approved.

The clarity of exterior expression continues inside. Under the roof is a bulbous and largely glass foyer, its shape seeming to come from carrying the load of the roof and in

Top left
Level 2: performers' dressing rooms surround the stage area.

Top right
Level 4: to the rear of the stage areas are large rehearsal studios and the canteen.

Bottom left
The west elevation faces the water: the design was
intended to have buildings flanking it on either side.

Bottom right
Cross-section.

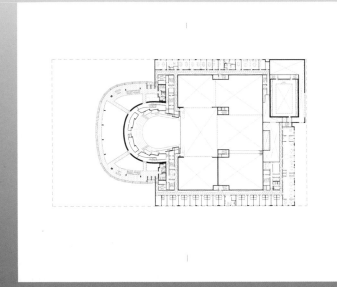

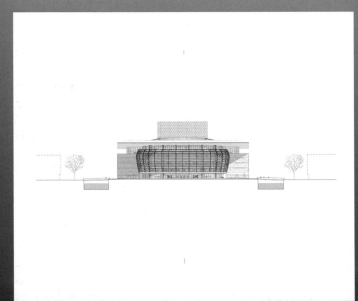

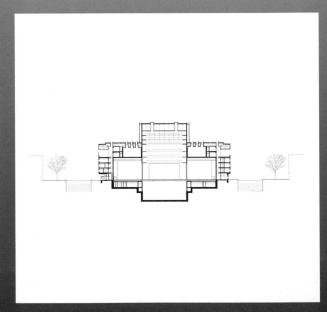

In the hands of British architects a space like that in the
Copenhagen Opera would become an excuse for another sort of
ostentatious, over-elaborate details or structural gymnastics, and
the message that opera-going in a Social Democracy – albeit one
where the Royal Family have their own entrance and floor, not unlike
the requirement that was foisted on Garnier for Napoleon III – could
genuinely appeal to all would have been diluted. But HLT keep the
appearance remarkably clean and crisp, rightly, as the drama of the
space needs no overstatement.

Top left and right
South elevation and longitudinal section: the long section resolves the generic conflicts of an
opera house, with foyer, auditorium, fly tower and backstage all neatly resolved under the
large roof.

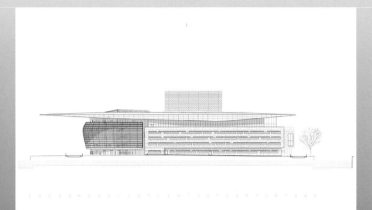

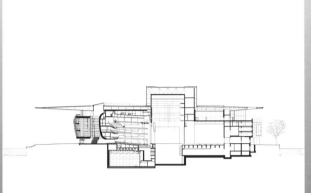

response to the curves of the auditorium rather than a whim. It is a wonderful space, taking advantage of 180-degree views on several levels, its several tiers linked by staircases and leading into the auditorium across bridges at a different angle on each level. In effect, the apparently floating planes and walkways have something of Asplund's Gothenburg Law Courts, or a less clumsy version of the Royal Festival Hall in London. But in its response to that necessary rite of opera-going, ostentatious display, it is also an update of Garnier's Opera in Paris, where even the most sumptuous crinolines and coiffeurs were lost against the opulent decoration and flow of space. In the hands of British architects, a space like that in the Copenhagen Opera would become an excuse for another sort of ostentatious, over-elaborate detail or structural gymnastics, and the message that opera-going in a social democracy – albeit one where the Royal Family have their own entrance and floor, not unlike the requirement that was foisted on Garnier for Napoleon III – could genuinely appeal to all would have been diluted. But HLT rightly keeps the appearance remarkably clean and crisp; the drama of the space needs no overstatement.

At the end of Wagner's *Das Rheingold* the gods, already suffering fearful premonitions that their twilight is only three nights away, enter Valhalla across a bridge cast by a rainbow. Entering the auditorium is not quite a simulacrum, but the bridges' precipitous positions, not stacked above each other but staggered, does induce a sense of transition from one world to another. A small lobby increases suspense, but then the auditorium opens: it has a sense of scale and occasion, with four tiers and stalls containing seats for 1,500 (or 1,700 in ballet mode), yet it is also intimate. Everywhere you look you can see faces. It is somewhere in the middle of the spectrum between the Met and Glyndebourne, but does suggest that there is a happy medium. Its combination of a horseshoe plan and considerable height gives it elegant proportions, and also helps to meet the client's original requirement: it maximises clear sightlines, keeps distances from stage and orchestra pit short, and gives the right volume for the best acoustic effects. It is also beautifully finished, with slotted timber fascias that again assist acoustic performance.

HLT falls very much within the tradition of Danish architecture, where beauty and satisfaction of functional requirements are considered to be more or less synonymous. In lesser hands, such an aim might seem trite, but when the function is as symbolically charged as opera there really can be a seamless transition from purpose to aesthetics. Opera will always evince controversy, at a banal level over its supposed elitism, and at a more serious level over whether its modalities really are powerful enough to suspend incredulity and take us straight to archetypal emotions. The architectural corollary to this is twofold: historical and contextual. The first question is whether a modern opera house can evince powerful operatic traditions and still resonate in the age of Vodafone Live; the second is whether so rarified a space as an operatic auditorium can fit meaningfully into the context of a modern city. HLT indicates a positive answer to both.

Having the best auditorium also means having superb stage and backstage facilities. At a basic level, HLT continues the theme of simplicity into the backstage areas. The stage is marked by a concrete enclosure, giving mass for acoustic separation and also indelibly marking its presence – an important consideration for visiting performers. The facilities are superb, with practice rooms of various sizes and a deep basement room with total acoustic separation, for soloists up to a full orchestra. This room, five stories below ground, has a timber finish and simulated natural light that could fool rehearsers into thinking they are in an agreeable Scandinavian forest. The stage, too, is outstanding. It is possible to have six different sets erected at the same time, with each moved into place for performances as required. This offsets the enormous cost of the frequent stage changes necessary because opera singers cannot perform on consecutive nights, into extra capital expenditure. ⌂+

Archer Architects, Soho Court housing scheme, Soho, London, ongoing
Below
Site plan. The site is in the heart of central London's West End, not far from
Piccadilly Circus.

Soho Court, London

Bruce Stewart describes how a patient and ever-persistent approach to planning have paid off for Archer Architects, the designers of a mixed-use housing scheme in the centre of London's Soho. The designers' considered response to 'community benefit' and the existing urban fabric have enabled them to overcome the stalemate on a site that has suffered from 'planners' blight' since the 1970s.

Top
Plan of the proposed development showing how the new
buildings replicate the existing morphology of the area.

Bottom
Denman Street elevation. The new elevation
will fit in with the existing grain of the street.

Soho Court, in the heart of London's West End, is one of the
largest new mixed-use redevelopment schemes in the area
for more than 30 years. Designed by Archer Architects, the
scheme was recently granted full planning approval by
Westminster City Council. The site, currently known as the
'Moulin site', is within a large city block bounded by Brewer
Street to the north, Great Windmill Street to the east, and
Denman Street to the south. Currently in a state of dereliction,
it has suffered from 'planners' blight' since the early 1970s.
Earmarked as a possible location for a new transport nexus,
any redevelopment proposals were met with a blanket refusal.
Its uncertain future has meant that the buildings within the
site – a factory and various other commercial units – have
fallen into disrepair and, currently, the main use of the site
is as a car park.

   Due to the 'blight' on the site it has been a very slow
process for the architects and the developers, the Shaw
Corporation, to win over the local authority and start to
regenerate this key urban location. Many discussions and a
variety of design proposals over more than four years have now
led to a scheme that will not only breathe new life into the
district but will lead the way for the continuing organic growth
of Soho. The planning office was very keen that Section 106 of
the planning policy documents play a key role in the evolution
of the design. This requires that a design provides 'community
benefit', which can take many forms including job creation,
educational initiatives, improving personal security and
upgrading the public realm.

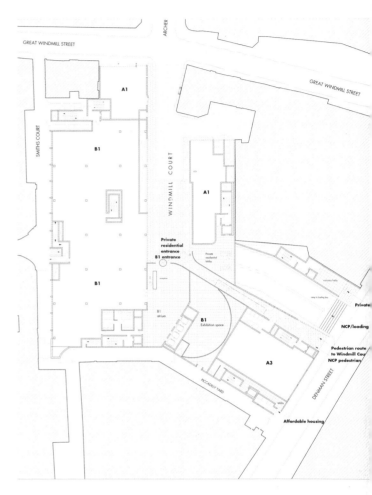

STRATEGIC VIEW LEVEL 27.127m

Below
Denman Gardens. The communal garden will link the three housing blocks to provide
private open space at first-floor level, creating a sense of community for the residents.

In order to fulfil the requirements of the developer, the planning department and the area, it was decided that none of the existing buildings will be retained in the redevelopment. This is not to say that the spirit and morphology of Soho is to be ignored. In fact, far from it; early analyses of the area have shown that there is a significant amount of a 'hidden' Soho – all the little alleys and courts that form the detailed grain of much of central London. This was a key point of the design's generation and growth. Alongside the physical grain of the city, another important factor that can affect design proposals throughout central London is the strategic viewing corridors that cross the city. These corridors mean that certain views from key points are protected by legislation; for example, the view from Greenwich to St Paul's Cathedral, and that from Primrose Hill across the city. The impact of the corridors is that there is a very definite height restriction on buildings like Soho Court that are erected in their path.

As mentioned, the site is mixed use and combines retail and office space with both private and public-sector housing. As such, there were many difficulties in formalising a scheme that responded to the need for both public urban space and the privacy that domestic buildings require. The solution was to create a new public 'court' at the heart of the site and split the accommodation into smaller individual buildings that would maintain the character of Soho yet add a rich new vibrancy.

The office space occupies the northern edge of the site bounded by Smiths Court, with the housing split into three blocks: one internal to Soho Court and the two remaining with frontages to Denman Street. A further difficulty was the need to not only maintain the existing car park but to include parking for all the new dwellings, both private and public sector. Alongside this are the new pressures created by adding more commercial space. The fabric of London is already dense, and lorries parking to make deliveries can create traffic nightmares. The solution to all these vehicular demands has been to create several basement levels that address all the issues. Loading and deliveries are made at the first of the basement levels, with residents parking and public parking below that, thus taking much of the stress away from the street itself.

At ground level there is retail space, and above this the domestic accommodation. By creating three new residential blocks, the texture of this central London site will complement the existing fabric of the neighbourhood, but it also raises a very delicate question: How are public- and private-sector housing requirements dealt with on a single site? There is a very strong push nowadays to provide public housing that does not have the nature of its tenant base described in

Below
The newly created court will add to the existing vibrancy of Soho and will be used
for public events such as the Soho Jazz Festival.

the architecture: poor quality = homes for poor people! It has been a requirement under the current government that where the number of units being built goes above a certain level, provision is made to include affordable homes to suit the needs of the local housing authority. Here, of 54 housing units, 21 are for the local housing association – Soho Housing. However, there can be differing spatial planning requirements between these two areas of the housing market. In the case of public housing, there are definite minimum standards for areas such as kitchens and storage (based on anthropological data) that may differ from those required by the market-driven private sector. Another factor is perceived 'need'. For example, in such a central, urban location as Soho Court, the private-sector need is for apartments and pied-à-terres, whilst the housing association need is for family homes and homes for key workers.

Archer Architects' solution could, at first glance, seem a little controversial. The current thinking is that in order to overcome any social stigmatisation, both types of provision need to be completely integrated with no visible separation. In Soho Court, the social housing is grouped in one of the three blocks with the private in the remaining two. However, this separation is based on the spatial planning differences that arose. In order to help with the provision of affordable homes, funding from the housing corporation is sought, and it is the corporation's guidelines that regulate the spatial standards within new affordable housing. At Soho Court, there will be no difference in the quality of the buildings in terms of materials and internal finishes. From street level upwards, the two blocks on Denman Street will have the same architectural vocabulary articulated in slightly different ways, which in itself is very much the nature of the district. And it is within the new court itself that it becomes especially clear that there is no desire to separate either public or private residents from each other. To create good, open private space for all the residents,

a large garden area is situated at the first-floor level and is seen as key to the integration of all the residents, being available to all with no sense of division, with equal access to this one large space from all three housing blocks.

Although it has been mentioned that separation of private and public-sector tenants is viewed as bad practice, it is more often than not the reality. In many cases, though the materials used may be the same, the positioning of the types of tenure within a site can lead to a definite identification of who is who. For example, the private-sector dwellings usually maximise any advantages the site has to offer, leaving the less attractive areas for public-sector provision. Fortunately, this is not the case in Soho Court; wherever possible, all units have a private external space alongside the communal garden. On Denman Street it is the private-, rather than the public-sector accommodation that is placed above the entrance to the lower-level parking. However, it must be stressed that, with a project of this scale and nature, there was never any desire to see any one element taking priority over the rest, and all decisions were therefore made based on lengthy discussions with all the interested parties.

The aim of the Soho Court development is to add to the vibrancy of the area by minimising the impact of traffic, increasing personal safety, providing a lively public space and creating new homes that will suit all those who live in the city. Δ+

SOHO COURT	G 0-29%	F 30-39%	E 40%	D 41-49%	C 50-59%	B 60-69%	A 70-100%
QUALITATIVE							
Space-Interior					C		
Space-Exterior						B	
Location							A
Community					C		
QUANTITATIVE							
Construction Cost				NA*			
Cost-rental/purchase				NA*			
Cost in use				NA*			
Sustainability				D			
AESTHETICS							
Good Design?						B	
Appeal						B	
Innovative?					C		

This table is based on an analytical method of success in contributing to solution to housing need. The criteria are: Quality of life – does the project maintain or improve good basic standards? Quantative factors – has the budget achieved the best it can? Aesthetics – does the building work visually?

Bruce Stewart, with Jane Briginshaw, is currently researching and writing *The Architects' Navigation Guide to New Housing*, to be published in autumn 2005 by Wiley-Academy. Bruce Stewart trained as an architect and is currently a college teacher at the Bartlett School of Architecture, UCL London.

realities:united, BIX installation, Kunsthaus Graz, Graz, Austria, 2004
Below
Designers' concept rendering of installation.

Blurring the Lines

Case Studies of Current CAD/CAM Techniques - BIX

The design of buildings is usually regarded as taking place before – or at latest during – their construction, yet arguably they continue to evolve via passive or active processes throughout their lifetimes, affected as they are by everything from the weather to occupant-induced modifications to responses by environmental control systems. Another, more overt kind of change is observable at the recently built Kunsthaus in Graz, Austria, where the BIX installation transforms the building's primary facade in accordance with programming by invited artists. This animated field of light fixtures both literally embodies an example of 'performative' architecture and foreshadows a whole range of potentially creative effects achievable through in-service alterations of a building's state, as posited by **André Chaszar** in this fifth instalment of Δ's 'Blurring the Lines' series of CAD/CAM case studies.

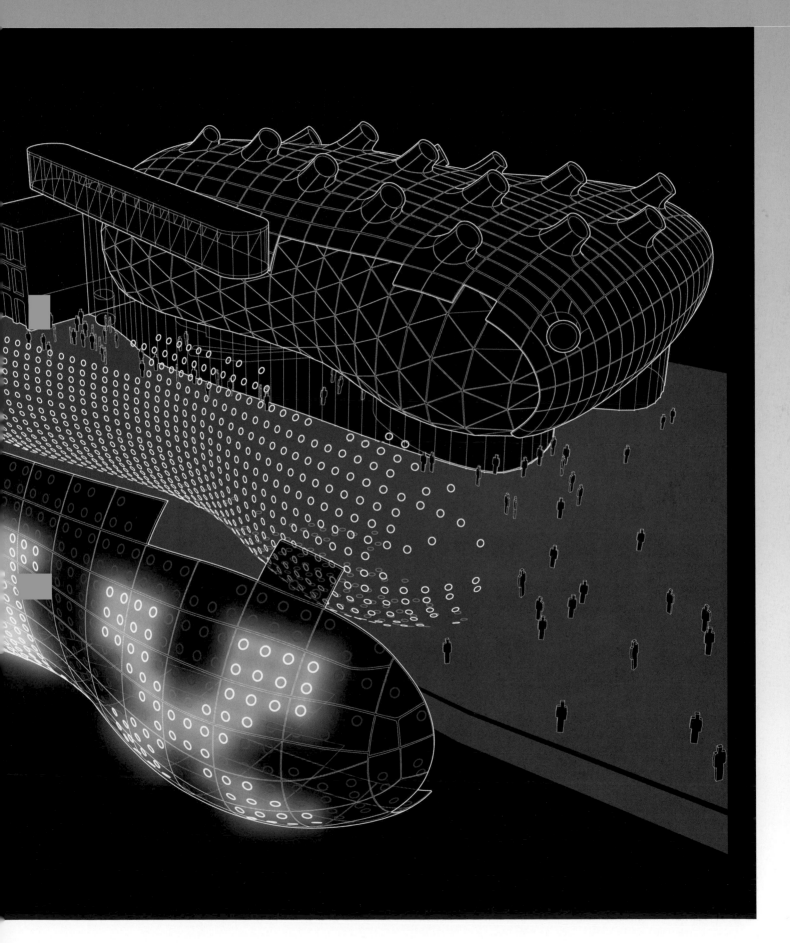

Top left
View of the Kunsthaus Graz and its environs with a video image on the BIX installation.

Bottom left
Close view of display field showing variously dimmed lamps.

Middle
Flattened map of pixel distribution.

Top right
Digital model showing details of BIX assembly and coordination with the facade system.

Rarely, if ever, does one see a building apparently caressing itself. Yet this and other remarkable effects have been achieved since the opening of the new contemporary art museum in Graz, through the efforts of architects realities:united of Berlin and of the artists who have utilised their BIX installation there – an installation commissioned as part of the museum's multimedia brief and realised as a permanent feature of the building's main facade. By enabling invited parties to screen video clips on a multistorey scale, the BIX installation brings a literal dynamism to architecture that transcends the long-familiar practice of commercial advertising on enormous electronic billboards and ushers in an age when designers may be able to bring their creativity to bear throughout the lifetimes of the buildings they have conceived.

Apparently to similar ends, much has been made in some architectural circles about 'performative effects', which –

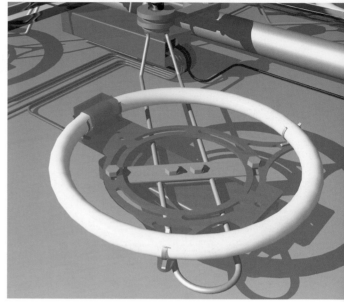

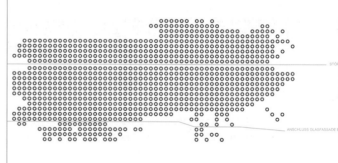

Top left
View of lamps with mountings, ballasts and wiring.

Right
Images from BIX software for editing and simulation of video installations, showing perspectival view, viewer location map and editing console.

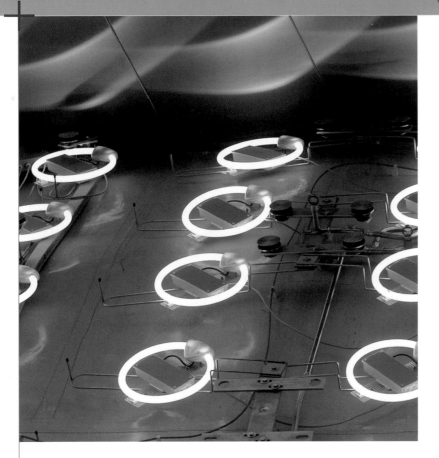

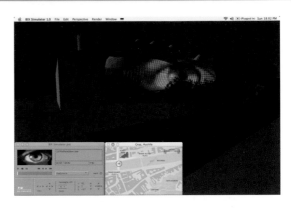

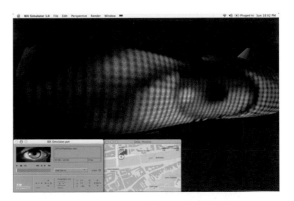

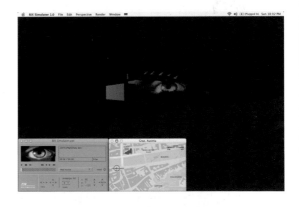

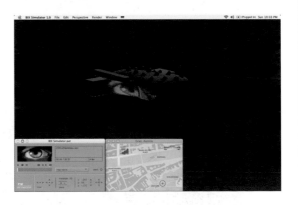

though no consensus has been reached regarding the meaning of the term – is generally understood as referring to literally dynamic phenomena affecting the architectural character of the building (if applied to a building). The phenomena may occur on various timescales, some perhaps even too slow to be immediately perceptible, and the effects that seem to elicit the greatest interest among designers are those involving some transformation of the architectural form. Thus, for example, exotic mechanically driven, undulating surfaces such as the Aegis Hyposurface (by dECOi, the Royal Melbourne Institute of Technology, Spacial Information Architecture Laboratory *et al*) qualify under this rubric, as would a number of contemporary interactive art installations.

Distinctions are subtle, though. The shadow of a passing cloud upon the building is apparently too passive, and nor have suggestions of the architectural value of extending and retracting awnings been greeted with much enthusiasm. (Perhaps, in fact, quite the opposite: consider Mies's reported objections to unruly, occupant-instigated patterns of window blinds on otherwise immaculate skyscrapers, and the general absence of such devices from architectural renderings even in our more enlightened present day.) While architectural response, delayed or real-time, to internal and/or external conditions might all be acceptable, the key prerequisite seems to be an element of choreography – setting aside for the moment the question of intention and whether the change is executed in a top-down or bottom-up manner.

Top
A series of stills from a video screening on the BIX installation.

Bottom
View of another moment in the video installation shown earlier.

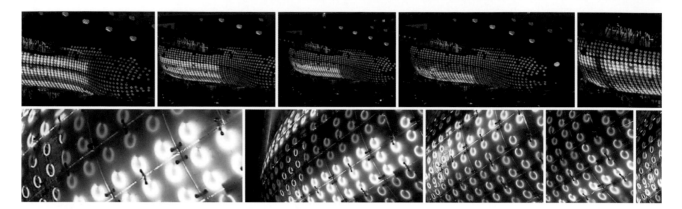

In the BIX installation, no mechanical action takes place, rather the building's surface becomes something like a very large video monitor. The image resolution is low, but the distinction between 'wall' and 'display' is thoroughly blurred by means of at least two moves: the embedding of the constituent light sources within exactly the same cladding system as covers most of the remaining building surface, and the termination of the display field not along a distinct boundary but a rough, seemingly random zone. These outcomes were driven partly by the project's budgetary and other logistical constraints, and partly by the desire of its designers to avoid any resemblance to a state-of-the-art system that would rapidly become obsolete due to the rapid advances now being made in the area of commercial large-scale video displays.

The physical components of the installation are relatively few and simple. The light sources are standard, toroidal fluorescent lamps mounted in the space between the building's transparent outer skin and the inboard waterproofed surface. Each lamp is individually controlled by a dimmable ballast, and the ballasts' controls are networked to a desktop computer that runs the show.

Digital design tools have been involved at a number of stages, from concept through execution and, most significantly, operation. As might by now be expected of projects showcased here, realities:united's interaction with the building's designers and the clients involved digitally prepared schematics, technical drawings and renderings, and the detailed development of the design included 3-D digital models of the system's components. In this instance, however, the designers went further by developing – in collaboration with programmers – a new software suite that provides an interface for programming the BIX installation and for simulating the resulting effect in the urban context. This was useful not only for the designers' own development of their concept and presentation to the clients, but also for the artists who have since been asked to prepare works for screening on the Kunsthaus Graz.

This operational aspect of the project potentially relates also to more widespread – and if more mundane, certainly not less important – performance aspects of buildings. Environmental, communications and security systems are increasingly handled by computerised facilities management and building management systems (BMS) hardware and software. These are characterised by distributed, as well as centralised computing, and some of the more advanced have predictive control and learning ability. While these systems are usually viewed as being normative, invisible technical apparatus beyond the realm of the architectural designer, through continued interest in performative aspects of architecture perhaps they could be turned to more aesthetic/cultural roles as well. Whether their extension in this way would be didactic, entertaining or otherwise in its aims, such a reconception might present enormous opportunities for realising truly dynamic built environments without falling back on clichéd consumer pyrotechnics, nor evoking fantasies of nanotechnologically self-building or self-repairing architectures, which though maybe plausible are inarguably out of reach for the present and near future. In this way we might even blur the lines between functional performance and play. △+

The author is an engineer with an independent consulting and research practice in New York. He is also a contributing editor of △ and serves on the △ editorial advisory board. This and other articles on the subject of CAD/CAM in architecture are collected in a book titled *Blurring the Lines*, scheduled for publication by Wiley-Academy later this year.

Charles and Adam Breeden with Fusion Architects, Lonsdale Bar, West London, 2003
Below
The bubble-cladding in the main bar is brass that has been treated to look like bronze. The Lonsdale was the first project by owner brothers Charles and Adam Breeden, who had a strong influence on the interior design.

Bubble Bar

Howard Watson describes how the Lonsdale Bar in West London has taken a 1970s Tardis-inspired vision of the future as the starting point for its very contemporary treatment.

For once an interior really can be described accurately as effervescent: much of the walls of London's Lonsdale Bar are clad with large metal bubbles. Sitting between the cool, moneyed and media-laden Ladbroke Grove and Westbourne Grove areas, just above London's Notting Hill, the Lonsdale's location meant that it was always likely to be popular, but the real crowd-puller is the highly unusual interior, which has had the design-savvy, cocktail cognoscenti humming with pleasure since the bar opened in January 2003. The pale blue, understated facade lies at the end of a quiet residential street. During the daytime, it is hard to imagine that it holds either such an exuberant, futuristic design or such a peerlessly hip clientele.

123+

Top
Genevieve, the private bar at the Lonsdale, features aluminium bubble-cladding on the walls and ceiling in homage to a 1970s vision of the future. The bubbles, custom-made by a metal-spinning company, reflect the lighting and offer a warped view of the interior.

Bottom
The low stools in the main bar are covered with 1970s-style, fun-fur textiles and velvets. The skylight is crafted out of specialised fibrous plaster. It steps up in rings of lighter colour, adding a planetary aspect to the sci-fi vision.

Working with Fusion Architects, with a budget of £2 million, brothers Charles and Adam Breeden created a design born out of a 1970s vision of the future: the Tardis would have looked like this had Doctor Who had an eye for interior design. The same design influences both the main Lonsdale public bar and the private Genevieve bar upstairs, but outside of its own four walls, it remains one of a kind. The outstanding features are the sections of bubble-cladding in both bars, which also extend onto the ceiling in Genevieve. In the public bar downstairs, the bubbles are made of brass, but have been treated to give the effect of bronze. Upstairs in Genevieve, the design is the same but the material is aluminium, giving the space a brighter, harder look.

The bubbles create an immediate design statement, marking the Lonsdale out from anywhere else, and it takes some time to realise the level of care that has gone into all aspects of the interior. Above the bar, for instance, the lights are made up of 80 layers of glass that create a graded purple rainbow effect, while a section of the downstairs bar ceiling is dotted with bubble impressions as if the bubble wall has been hinged down from it. One of the more dominant features of the downstairs interior is the atrium-like skylight. Constructed from specialised, fibrous plaster it is made up of a telescoping series of rings that increase in brightness as if reaching towards a planet's white-hot core.

Returning to earth, the bar counters in both spaces, as well as the stairs in between, are covered in fossilised limestone. This is also used for the flooring of the main bar. All the banquettes are covered with premium hide, while the funky, retro 1970s look is further invigorated by a mixture of fun-fur patterns on the low stools. These serve to add a little disorganised, sexy fun to the interior, just in case one feels that it takes itself too seriously. The tables they surround are made from solid teak, sourced from protected forests.

Charles Breeden chose to work with Fusion Architects based on the practice's designs for Momo restaurant with Mourad Mazouz, who went on to open Sketch. A great fan of Momo, Breeden also used the restaurant's audio-visual contractor, Sound Division Group. Music plays an important part of the ambience at the Lonsdale, but Breeden wanted a discreet, as well as powerful, sound system that could be regulated independently over the venue's three floors. Sound Division Group set up the DJ area with an advanced Allen & Heath Xone 62 mixer and installed a large video screen and projector in Genevieve.

The intimate atmosphere in both spaces is helped by the fact that the brothers Breeden continue to have a hands-on approach, and not just with regard to the design; they are still regularly seen at the bar. They have created a unique interior that readily lends itself to the ongoing cocktail sophistication that has swept London since the mid-1990s. The cocktails have their own designer, Dick Bradsell, who is probably second only to Salvatore Calabresi in the list of London's greatest living mixologists. Further accreditation for the venture has come from Selfridge's, the department store that in recent years has been trying to associate itself (sometimes somewhat desperately) with the best of radical, contemporary art and design; the Breedens have created a mini-Lonsdale within the new men's superbrands section, which opened in 2004. ⚙+

Howard Watson is an author, journalist and editor living in London. His book, *Bar Style: Hotel and Members' Bars*, charting the international revitalisation of bar design, will be published by Wiley-Academy in spring 2005.

Standen National Trust property , West Sussex (1891)
Middle
South front.

Right
East wall of the dining room and major bedroom.

Philip Webb: Pioneer of Arts & Crafts Architecture

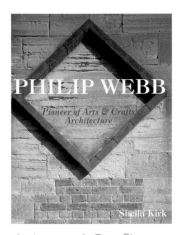

Arts and Crafts architecture has reached an important turning point in its reassessment. The 'International Arts and Crafts' exhibition opens at the V&A in London from 17 March to 24 July 2005 (before travelling on to the Indianapolis Museum of Art in autumn this year, and the de Young Museum in San Francisco in spring 2006). Coinciding with this is Wiley-Academy's publication of the first definitive monograph of leading Arts and Crafts architect Philip Webb (1831–1915). This long-awaited book, by architectural historian **Sheila Kirk**, includes specially commissioned photography by Martin Charles. Interweaving biography with evocative descriptions of all of Webb's seminal buildings, Kirk perceptively breathes life into one of the quietest members of William Morris's circle, and provides a new understanding of the buildings of a man who offered strong principles and firm guidelines yet at the same time allowing ample freedom of design. Here, she describes the relevance of Webb's national vernacular approach for architecture today.

Philip Webb had a passionate love for medieval architecture, vernacular houses and the English countryside, and was appalled by the adverse effects of industrialisation on these. In 1859, when he set up practice in London, his peers were obsessed with revivals of past styles or the possibility of creating a new style for the age. Although influenced to some degree by the writing of Ruskin and the work of the Gothic revivalists Pugin, Street and William Butterfield, Webb had concluded that all style revivals degraded architecture, and that when under commercial pressures architects began a revival during the Renaissance, they had become divorced from the realities of building, with the result that by his own day they lacked the essential knowledge of materials and construction. Architecture had become a mechanical affair of cribs and exhibition drawings instead of a living, developing tradition of good building. Webb had no wish to celebrate the industrial age,

and believed that a completely new style was an impossibility, as ideas and designs could develop only from what already existed, and therefore all new buildings must necessarily contain something of the past. He resolved to make his architecture a matter of excellent building, fitting for the climate and other national and local characteristics, in the hope that other architects, in other countries, would do likewise.

By the 1860s, Webb had a vast knowledge of English buildings of all types and sizes, and of materials and how they could be worked and used, in addition to how well they would weather. This was essential to his approach, of which the key words and phrases are simplicity, common sense, reason and practicality, and the truthful expression of materials, methods of construction and the function of the building. He provided a first-class professional service – a convenient plan being of primary importance – and adjusted practical details to suit the wishes of his clients, though insisting on retaining design autonomy. He believed it was essential to approach each commission with an open mind, without preconceived notions of the likely appearance of the new building, and that an architect must protect the landscape, in town or country, by avoiding ostentatious, self-advertising designs and ephemerally fashionable elements, and by ensuring that new buildings would weather pleasingly. He designed every detail of his buildings himself, in order to create a consistent whole.

Webb exploited the possibilities of a site, allowing its character to partially determine that of the building and its topography, to assist in making the new structure unobtrusive. Though he reflected the character of the local vernacular, he made inventive experiments in the use of materials to avoid stagnation and to add to the building tradition. In his work, movement, contrasts of controlled irregularity with symmetry and rhythm, contrasts of size, light and shadow, and of the varying colours and textures of materials, replaced style motifs. Regarding as a fallacy Ruskin's assertion that a building without ornament is not architecture, and finding contemporary ornament lifeless, he omitted it in his smaller buildings and limited it in his larger ones. Believing over-plainness to be as ostentatious as over-elaboration, however, he avoided this by increasing the number of details such as strings, architraves and cornices. He adopted new methods and new materials only when they improved on traditional counterparts and where their use would be in harmony with nearby existing buildings.

In addition, Webb often used an appropriate national building type, such as a 13th-century quadrangular castle, an Elizabethan prodigy house or a Border pele, as the 'idea', the inspiration that governed his early thoughts about the appearance of a new building, but which is seldom identifiable in the final structure. Standen (1891), a country house near East Grinstead in West Sussex, for which Compton Wynyates, an early 16th-century courtyard house, formed the idea, is an excellent exemplar of what Webb achieved with his national vernacular approach. Δ+

Philip Webb: Pioneer of Arts & Crafts Architecture, by Sheila Kirk, with photographs by Martin Charles (Wiley-Academy, 2005) is available in hardback (ISBN: 0-471-98708-5) at £60.00, and paperback (ISBN: 0-470-86808-2) at £29.99, from www.wiley.com.

Also available:
*Baillie Scott
The Artistic House*
by Diane Haigh
(ISBN: 0-470-86808-2).

The London Stone Show 2005
Wembley Exhibition Centre
5–7 April

The London Stone Show is the UK's renowned international natural stone show, during which top manufacturers and suppliers of natural stone and ancillary products are able to showcase their materials to the UK market.

Focusing on architectural and building stone, with a section dedicated to quality hard coverings, the show provides an integrated visitor experience for architects.

It is now in its third year, and is a magnet for thousands of visitors who want to source stone and stone-related products for use in, on or around buildings. 'We have a strong business-to-business forum with an established track record that attracts exhibitors from around the world,' says Mark Palmer, managing director of the show. 'We have moved to a bigger venue to cope with the increased demand for both exhibition space and visitor numbers. This year sees us at Wembley Exhibition Centre for the first time, with over 17,000 metres of exhibition space and room for over 3,000 cars.'

Over the three days, more than 300 exhibitors, including Ansum Ash/TAB India, Antolini Luigi, Ardex, Bagnara Nikolaus, Degussa Chemicals, Grein Italia, Johann Steigler, Mapei, Marbonyx, Marsotto, Milcomar and Stoneville, will be exhibiting their high-quality products.

Featuring thousands of new and innovative natural stone products from more than 20 countries, the depth and variety on display will provide visitors with a one-stop-show where they can view and source materials.

To register to attend the UK's premier stone exhibition, or for further information, please visit www.thestoneshow.com, or contact +44 (0)1442 828173.

london **stone** show ⁰⁵

opening the door to the world of stone

The Natural Choice for Professionals in Stone...

Wembley Exhibition Centre, UK

April 5th-7th 2005

Learn about the new trends and technologies available to the stone industry from the show that brings a wealth of knowledge to the UK market place

See over 300 natural stone producers from around the world exhibiting products of the highest quality

Source from the spectacular variety and natural beauty of products on display

Visit www.thestoneshow.com or call 01442 828173 to pre-register for free entrance to the show, or alternatively pay only £5.00 entrance fee on the day.

Bringing fresh ideas to the UK market place

7016